ISBN 978-1-331-95777-5
PIBN 10259629

1 MONTH OF
FREE
READING

at
www.ForgottenBooks.com

By purchasing this book you are eligible for one month membership to ForgottenBooks.com, giving you unlimited access to our entire collection of over 700,000 titles via our web site and mobile apps.

To claim your free month visit:
www.forgottenbooks.com/free259629

English
Français
Deutsche
Italiano
Español
Português

www.forgottenbooks.com

Mythology Photography **Fiction**
Fishing Christianity **Art** Cooking
Essays Buddhism Freemasonry
Medicine **Biology** Music **Ancient
Egypt** Evolution Carpentry Physics
Dance Geology **Mathematics** Fitness
Shakespeare **Folklore** Yoga Marketing
Confidence Immortality Biographies
Poetry **Psychology** Witchcraft
Electronics Chemistry History **Law**
Accounting **Philosophy** Anthropology
Alchemy Drama Quantum Mechanics
Atheism Sexual Health **Ancient History**
Entrepreneurship Languages Sport
Paleontology Needlework Islam
Metaphysics Investment Archaeology
Parenting Statistics Criminology
Motivational

The Registers

OF

Boughton-under-Blean.

CO. KENT.

Issued By
THE PARISH REGISTER SOCIETY.
(XLIX.)

The Registers

OF

Boughton-under-Blean,

CO. KENT.

BAPTISMS ...	...	1558—1624
MARRIAGES ...	...	1558—1626
BURIALS ...	...	1558—1625

TRANSCRIBED BY THE VICAR

THE REV. JOHN ADOLPHUS BOODLE, M.A.

CONTENTS

P

Kent B

LONDON :

PRIVATELY PRINTED FOR THE PARISH REGISTER SOCIETY.

1903.

PREFACE.

The earliest Register of the Parish of Boughton-under-Blean is a parchment volume, measuring 18½ inches by 6¾ inches and containing one hundred pages, fifty folios, of which forty-seven are covered with entries. The purchase of this book is recorded in the Churchwardens' Accounts for 1598 in the following terms: "Ite. for a Register book of parchment xii*s*," and the accuracy of the transcripts of the entries up to that date is testified by the signatures of Wm. Place (Vicar of Boughton 17th March, 1589, to his death in 1637—buried April 7th) and Richard Rucke, one of the Churchwardens, and the mark of Thomas Hendman the other Churchwarden.

The Baptisms are recorded from 3rd April, 1558, to 20th June, 1624, with a hiatus from 9th January, 157$\frac{0}{1}$ to 23rd November, 1571; the Marriages from 14th June, 1558, to 15th May, 1626, with a hiatus from 28th December, 1570, to 9th June, 1572; and the Burials from 1st April, 1558, to 15th March, 162$\frac{5}{6}$, with a hiatus from 8th January, 157$\frac{0}{1}$, to 19th November, 1571.

The writing is for the most part legible, so that there are very few words which it has not been possible to decipher.

RECTORS AND VICARS.

The principal Manor and Church of Boughton under the Blean ("Bocton subtus le Bleyn" as it is styled in the old Church Book dating from 1534) are among the most ancient possessions of the See of Canterbury, the Archbishop being mentioned in Doomsday Book as holding the lands himself.

Before the year 1340 the Archbishop appointed the Rector of Boughton, and the Rector appointed a Vicar, as well as a Chaplain to the dependant Chapelry of Hernhill. But on 3 April 1340 the Rectorial Tithes and the Rectory House were exchanged by Archbishop Stratford with the Abbey of Faversham for other lands. At the Dissolution of Religious Houses in 1538 these Tithes, with the other revenues of Faversham Abbey, were seized by King Henry VIII, who by his dotation charter in 1541 settled them upon his newly-appointed Dean and Chapter Canterbury. In recent times these Tithes passed to the Ecclesiastical Commissioners, but have been re-transferred by them to the Dean and Chapter. As a part of Archbishop Stratford's transaction with Faversham Abbey, he retained for the Archiepiscopal See the patronage of the Vicarage of Boughton as well as the patronage of Hernhill, which was then constituted a Vicarage.

Date of Collation.	*Rectors.*	*Vicars.*
— June 1207.	Wuluinus, "Clericus Comitis Flandriæ."	
31 Oct. 1228.	Ranulphus Brito (or le Breton) [Preb. of Cadington Major in St. Paul's Cath., 1228. Rector of Layham, Suffolk, 1228. Preb. (*sic*) of Charing, Kent, 1228. Rector of Bocton, Kent, 1228. Preb. of Sarum, ——. Dean of Wimborne Minster, Dorset, elected 12 Oct. 1229. Died of an apoplexy, 1246. ("Novum Repertorium," by Hennessy, and Hutchins' "Hist. of Dorset.")	
8 Dec. 1270.	Egidius de Audenard. [Pat. 55 Henry III, *m.* 26.]	
——	Nicholas de Knovyle, presented William de Schoreham to Chapelry of Harenhulle 8 Id. Oct. 1283, and presented Rogerus *dictus* Dobbe to this Chapelry 13 Kal. Nov. 1285, and presented Johannes de Charleton to Vicarage of Boughton 13 Kal. Nov. 1285.	1285 Johannes de Charleton.
——	Gilbert de Sancto Leofardo. [Reg. Peckham, f. 37b.]	
5 Non. Jul. 1288.	William de Sardynia, juris civilis professor, per resig. G. de S.L. [Preb. of Welton Beckhall and Welton Brinkhall in Lincoln Cath. Preb. of Colwall in Hereford Cath. Preb. of Bitton in Salisbury Cath. Preb. of Timberbury in Romsey Abbey. Preb. of Ealdstreet in St. Paul's Cath., 1271—1303. Archdeacon of Oxford, 1297—	

ollation.	*Rectors.*	*Vicars.*
	1299. Preb. of Islington in St. Paul's Cath., 1303. Vicar of Goodnestone, Kent, 29 July 1282. Rector of Gt. Chart, Kent, 1283. Rector of Chiddingstone, Kent, Nov. 1283. Canon of Wingham (Chilton), Feb. 1287. Rector of Boughton with Chapel of Hern Hill, July 1288. Official of the Arches Court. Died 5 Nov. 1303, at Sarden (*sic*), near Canterbury, where he was buried. When Archbishop Peckham, in Nov. 1282, went into Wales to try to arrange peace between Llewelyn and Edward I, William de Sardenia was one of those appointed to look after the rights of the Archbishop during his absence.	
311.	Henry de Derby. [Reg. Winchelsey, f. 50a].	
. 1313.	Thomas de Leycester, admitted on presentation of the King, *sede vacante.* Still in office in Nov. 1322.	7 Id. Mart. 131½ Thomas Edm. de Faversham [called Thomas Monde,
	Jordan de Caunvyll, mentioned 6 Nov. 1325 [Close Roll, 19 Edward II, *m.* 24d] exchanged with Philip de Turvyll, 2 Jan. 132⅞ [Pat. 1 Edward III, pt. 3, *m.* 4].	Kent Fines, 8 Edward II.]
2⅞.	Philip de Turvyll. Richard Meopham? [Hasted].	

VICARS.

4 Aug. 1349.	John de Stony Stretford. [Pat. 23 Edward III, pt. 2, *m.* 16.]
11 Kal. Aug. 1353.	Laurentius de Beklesfeld (or Bekenesfeld) apud Magdenestan [exchanged with Richard Andrewe, Vicar Capellae B.M. infra Castrum de Chilham].
8 Id. Aug. 1359.	Richard Andrewe, per resig. L. de B. apud Otteford [exchanged with Robert Newman, Vicar of Folkestone].
6 Kal. Nov. 1360.	Robert Newman, per resig. R.A. [exchanged with John Langwath, Rector of Streete, Cyc. (*i.e.*, Chichester) Dioc].
17 Kal. Jan. 1363.	John Langwath, per resig. R.N. [exchanged with John Langham, Rector of St. Mary Magdalen, Canterbury, 1382].
8 Nov. 1382.	John Langham, per resig. J.L.
2 Oct. 1384.	Richard Shene, by exchange with J.L.
——	John Bowyer [exchanged with John Whitman, Vicar of Sydyngborne, 1402].
22 June 1402.	John Whitman, per resig. J.B. [exchanged with Lawrence Strenge, Rector of Otryndenn, (Otterden), 1410].
9 Feb. 1410.	Lawrence Strenge, per resig. J.W.
——	Giles Cassell [Hasted].
— 1456.	Peter Ellis [Hasted].
——	William Wayte.
——	Thomas Houghton [exchanged with Thomas Bateman, Rector of St. Margaret Pattens, London, 1479].
16 Sep. 1479.	Thomas Bateman, per resig. T.H.
— 1497.	John Barber [Hasted].
——	John Benyngton.
10 Nov. 1501.	John Belle, S.T.B., per mort. J.B.
— 1506?	Adam Browne [Hasted].
— 1526?	Edward Sponar, referred to in old Church Book as Vicar in 1536 [Rector of St. Swithin's, London, 1548-49. Died 1549. Nov. Rep.].
13 Jan. 1548.	Edward Layton, S.T.P., per resig. E.S. [Qy. if Preb. of Westminster, 17 Dec. 1540 to 20 April 1547. Nov. Rep.]. 3rd stall.

49.   John Huntyngdon, per mort. E.L.
1.   Roger Lymsey, per resig. J.H.
54.   Robert Thompson.
74.   George Bassett, per resig. R.T. [Curate of
        Whitstable. Rector of Swalecliffe in 1569].
76.   Albert Bassett, per resig. G.B. [Curate of
        Luddenham in 1569, Rector of Swaylecliffe,
        1575-87. Rector of Luddenham, 1580-87].
87.   Thomas Taylor, per mort. A.B. [Deprived
        for non-residence, 10 March 1589.]
589.   William Place.
7.   Samuel Smith, per mort. W.P. [Is referred
        to as Vicar on 9 Feb. 1640-41, in list of
        charges against him laid before the Committee
        of Religion appointed by Parliament.]
        Richard Harding, appointed by Committee of
        Parliament on sequestration of S.S.
6.   John Baker, per resign. R.H.
        Mr. Hercules Hill, minister ["Augmentation
        of Church Lands"].
        Mr. Thomas Seyliard ["Augmentation of
        Church Lands"]. [A Presbyterian, but
        B.A. of Jesus Coll., Cambridge, ordained
        Deacon by Bp. of Ely, 18 Dec. 1682.
        Obtains letters of dimission from Archbishop,
        21 Dec. 1682, to be ordained Priest by
        Bp. of Ely " the next solemn day of ordin-
        ation," granted by fiat 21 Dec. 1682.]
        John Dalton, Clerk, M.A., admitted upon
        a presentment exhibited by William Ken-
        wrick, Esq., the patron being at the same
        time approved by the Commissioners for
        approbation · of public preachers. ["Aug-
        mentation of Church Lands."]
        John Mackallar. (?)
o.   Magister Philip Holland. [Son of Philip of
        Macclesfield, Cheshire, sacerdotus. Brase-
        nose Coll., matric. 9 Dec. 1631, æt, 18.
        B.A., 13 Feb. 1633-34. Rector of Willey,
        Warw., 1639, and perhaps Vicar of Boughton-

under-Blean, Kent, 1660. Vicar of Cavers-
field, Bucks, 1661, and of Orpington, Kent,
1663. Foster's "Alumni Oxonienses."]

53. Percival Radcliffe, died 10 Sept. 1666. [B.A.
from New Inn Hall, 4 July 1626, perhaps
served cure of St. Bees, Camb. 1647.
Another of same name was Vicar of Boughton
under Blean, Kent, 1663. Foster's "Alumni
Oxonienses."]

David Barton, sequestered Boughton.

Robert Skene, Vicar of Hernhill, sequestered
Boughton, fiat dated 6 June 1671.

John Gamlyn, Vicar of Hernhill, sequestered
Boughton, Vicar of Faversham, 12 Aug.
1682. Vicar of Preston by Faversham, June
1684. Buried at Boughton, 17 June 1715.

Thomas Allen, Vicar of Hernhill and seques-
trator of Boughton.

John Johnson, on death of Thomas Allen,
Vicar of Hernhill, 12 April 1690. M.A.,
C.C.C., Cambridge, 1685. Vicar of Apple-
dore cum cap. de Ebony, 1 May 1697, and
Vicar of St. John's, Thanet, by sequestration.
Vicar of Cranbrook, 13 April 1707. Died
15 Dec. 1723. Buried at Cranbrook.

97. John Conold, per cess. J.J.

04. William Plees, per mort. J.C. M.A., C.C.C.,
Cambridge. Vicar of Hernhill, 3 March
170⅘.

52. Henry Heaton, per mort. W.P. B.D., C.C C.,
Cambridge. Vicar of Hernhill.

7. Stanhope Ellison, per mort. H.H. [M.A. St.
John's, Camb., 1761. Vicar of Thorpe,
Surrey. Rector of Wimbish, Essex. Rector
of St. Benet's, Paul's Wharf, 1757-74.
Novum Rep.]

Charles Moore, per mort. S.E. M.A., Trin.
Coll., Camb. Vicar of Cuxton.

3. Thomas William Wrighte, M.A., per resig.
C.M. Rector of Witching, 7 April 1795.

Samuel George Booth White, per mort. T.W.W.
M.A., Caius Coll., Cambridge. Rector of
Stansted, Kent, 1846.

Edward Henry Lee, per mort S.G.B.W. [4th son
of William, of Newington, Surrey, arm.
New Inn Hall, Ox., matric. 27 May 1837,
æt. 27; B A., 1841 (as Henry Edward), Curate
in Charge, Cliffe at Hoo, Kent, 1850-69,
Vicar of Boughton-under-Blean, 1869-75,
Rector of Chiddingstone since 1875. Foster's
" Alumni Oxonienses."]

75. Henry Maxwell Spooner, per. cess. E.H.L.
[2nd son of William, of Elmdon, Warw.,
arm. Balliol Coll , Ox., matric., 4 April
1864, æt. 17, Exhibitioner, 1864-68. Fellow
of Magdalene Coll., 1868-76. B.A., 1868.
M.A., 1871. Vicar of Boughton-under-
Blean, Kent, 1875-1887. Vicar of Holy
Trinity, Maidstone, 1887—1893 Rector of
Saltwood, Hythe, Kent, 1893-1900. Resid.
Canon of Canterbury. Archdeacon of Maid-
stone from 1900. Foster's " Alumni.
Oxonienses."]

7. John Adolphus Boodle, per cess. H.M.S.
M.A., St. John's Coll., Camb. Curate of
Buckingham, 1859-61. Curate of W. Mall-
ing, 1867-87. Vicar of Boughton-under-Blean
1887. Rural Dean of Ospringe from 1897.

Boughton=under=Blean Register.

On the outside of cover.

A Booke for ye Parish of Boughton under ye bleene in ye
Dioces of Canterbury Deanery of Ospringe from ye yeare
of God 1558.

On the inside of cover.

. . . xi^{li} vnto John Bo . . . of the pishe of St Laurence in Thanet
yeomn̄ to be paid in or on the feast daie of St John ye
Evangelest next at or in ye west porch as fforsaid.

1625.

the 9th of april baptised . . . wood . . . of Richard wood.

On the flyleaf.

16 of January buryed R.M.
21 of ffebr̄ . . . bur^d.
28 of ffebruary An Bayley, James Baker bap.
7 March ba. Mary Hilles.

Robert Ayres about . . . betwene 30 & 42.

A Register of the Christenings
Marriages & Burialls that habe
bin in the p'ish of Boughton under
the bleane ffrom the beginning
of ye first yere of the Raigne
of our Soberaigne Ladie Queen
Elizabethe etc.

Here beginnethe the yere of our Lord 1558   1558.

Christenings.

The third day of Aprill was baptized Laurenc' Morton.
The xxvith of Aprill was baptized Marke Juce.
The iij^d of May was baptized Avis Juce.
The xvth of May was baptized Mildred Essex.
The xxth of May was bapt^d John Hills.
The xxiith of May was bapt^d Alice Smyth.
The 18^{tb} of August was bapt^d Marie Pettit.

B

The 28th of August was bapt^d John Clifford.
The xth of September was baptiz. Robert Smyth.
The xvth of Septēb. was bapt^d Rychard ffuller.
The last of Septēb. was bapt^d John Tennaker.
The first of October was bapt^d Jean Dod.
The ii^d of Octoƀ was bapt^d John Pemble.
The 26th of Octoƀ was bapt^d John Shroubsoll.
The xviith of Nouēb. was bapt^d Steven Hunt.
The first of Decēber was baptiz. Edw: Harman.
The xth of Decēber was bapt^d Mathew Adie.
The xiith of Decēbe. was bapt^d Margaret Kyng.
The first of Januarie was bapt^d John Joans.
The xixth of Januarie was bapt^d Tho : Edwards.
The xxxth of Jan. was bapt^d John Carter.
The last of Januarie Margaret . . . was bapt^d.

Here entreth the yere of our Lord 1559.
The xvth of May was bapt^d Agnes Shroubsoll.
The 18th of June was bapt^d Phillyp Place.
The 6th of August was bapt^d Edward Bruke.
The same day was bapt^d James Anker.
The xxviith of of August was bapt^d John Bayley.
The xvth of Septēber was bapt^d Henrie Dūkin.
The ffirst of Octob^r was bapt^d Edward Howesse.
The xvth of Octob^r was bapt^d Edward Shroubsoll.
The 12th of November was bapt^d Edw. Place.
The third of December was bapt^d Ellen Berrie.
The same day was bapt^d Elizabeth Goddard.
The same day was bapt^d Elizabeth Poredge.
The 28th of Decēber was bapt^d Thomas Brise.
The 6th of Januarie was bapt^d Avis Lull.
The 4th of ffeb. was bapt^d Edward Juce.
The seconnd of ffeb. was bapt^d Florence Songer.
The xvth of ffeb. was baptized Ann Tennaker.

Here entreth the yere of our Lord 1560.
The last of March was bapt. Agnes Drury.
The xviith of Aprill was bapt. Ann Clifford.
The xixth of May was bapt. . . . Wernam.
The xxiiith of May baptized Ann Essex.
The same day was bapt^d Avis Shroubsoll.
The xxvith of May was bapt^d Alicè Rayner.
The xxviith of May was bapt^d Joan Turner.
The seconnd of June was bapt^d Cirriack Rucke.
The third of June was bapt^d John Best.
The third of July was bapt. Joan Hammon.

WILLIAM PLACE.
RICHARD RUCK.
THOMAS HENDMAN, hys mark ⊕

Page 2.

The same day was baptized Ralf . . .
The xiiith of July was bapt. Joan Cornish.
The xxvth of August was bapt^d Dennis Juce.
The xvth of Septēb^r was bapt^d John Kyng.
The xxiith of Septēber was bapt^d Avis Joans.
The ivth of Octob^r was bapt^d Edward Pettyt.
The 24th of Novēb^r was bapt^d Joan Vigars.
The xviith of Novēber was bapt^d Marg^y Shrobsoll.
The 24th of Novēb^r was bapt^d John Curthop.
The xxviiith of December was bapt^d Marg^y Brooke.
The vth of Januarie was bapt^d Thomas Hāmon.
The viiith of Jan. was bapt^d Avis Prior.
The 12th of Jan. was bapt^d Susan Shroubsoll.
The xxvith of Jan. was bapt^d Julyan Onings.
The third of ffeb^r was bapt^d Stephen Blackborne.
The last of Januarie was bapt^d John the sonne of a stranger.
The 2^d of March bapt^d Ann Hills.

Here entrethe the yere of our Lord 1561.

The 26th of March was bapt^d Susan Shroubsoll.
The xixth of May was bapt^d John Place, Ju.
The ffirst of June was bapt^d Joan Juce.
The 8th of June was bapt^d Margerie Best.
The xvth of June was bapt^d Alice Penystone.
The 8th day of July was bapt^d Marg^e Blunkett.
The xxiiith of Julye was bapt^d Tho : ffaireman.
The xth of August was bapt^d Avis Clyfford.
The last of August was bapt^d Robt. Norman.
Nicholas Howlet *alias* Hāmond was bapt^d the xiiijth of September.
The xxvith of Septēb^r was bapt^d Joan Dunkin.
The xxixth of Septēb^r was bapt^d Christian Chaplyne.
The xxiith of Octob bapt^d Edw· Dod.
The same day was bapt^d Henrie Porredg.
The xiith of October was bapt^d Barbara Lull.
The xiith of Novēb. was bapt^d Edward Layton.
The 7th of Novēb. was bapt^d Elizabeth Juce.
The 25th of Decēb^r was bapt^d Joan Tennaker.
The 4th of Januarie was bapt^d Lucye Goddard.
The 23th of Januarie was bapt^d Joan Songer.
The 20th of ffeb was bapt^d John Collyns.
The 23th of ffeb was bapt^d Avis Smith.
The 8th of March was bapt^d Marg^e Brooke.
The xth of March was bapt^d Margaret Shrobsoll.

Here entreth the yere of our Lord 1562.

The xiiith of Aprill was bapt^d Mathew Showter, son of a stranger.
The last of May bapt^d Barbara Howesse.
B²

The seconnd of August was bapt^d Wm Best.
The xvi^th of August was bapt^d Richard Carter.
The 8th of Septēb. was bapt^d Cciriak Jacob.
The xiii^th of Septēb. was bapt^d Stephan Spencer.
The xv^th of Septēb. was bapt^d John Shroubsoll.
The xi^th of Octoƀ was bapt^d Dennis Kyng.
The xxviii^th of Octoƀ was bapt^d florence Throwley.
The 8th of Novēh. was baptized Elizab : Snode.
The 8 of Novēb. was bapt^d Avis Cornish.
The 6th of Decēb. was bapt^d Catharine Hunt.
The 20th of Decēb. was bapt^d Joan Shroubsoll.
The 21th of Decēb. was bapt^d Rychard Rucke.

WILLIAM PLACE.
RICHARD RUCK.
THOMAS HENDMAN. ⊕

Page 3.

The xiiij^th of ffeb. was bapt^d Ann Songer the Daughter of Edward Songer.
The same daie was bapt. Alice Joans.
The 21th of ffeƀ was bapt^d Margaret Essex.
The 24th of feƀ was bapt^d Mathew ffaireman.
The 3^d of March was bapt. Daniell Tylman.

Here entreth the yere of our Lord 1563.

The 12th of May was bapt. Joseph Porredg the sonne of Stephan Porredge.
The xiiij^th of May was bapt^d Joan Curthop the daught^r of John Curthop.
The 24th of May was baptized Stephan Juce the sonne of Wm Juce.
The 24th of June was bapt. Joan May the Daughter of John May.
The 27th of June was bapt. Ann Collyns the Daughter of John Collens.
The xth day of July was baptized Henrie Hammond the sonne of Richard Hammond.
The xix^th daie of July was bapt. William Hammon the sonne of Edward Hammon.
The xi^th of August was bapt. Dorcas Denslade.
The 24th of August was bapt^d Thomsyn Porredg.
The 4th of Septēb. was bapt^d John Lull.
The 8th of Septēb. was bapt^d Ellis Juce.
The xv^th of Septēb. was baptized ffaith Norman.
The 23th of Septēb. was bapt. John Blunkett.
The xxix^th of Sept. was bapt. Margaret friar.
The 4th of October was bapt^d Marg' Laurence.
The xxiiij of Octoƀ was bapt. Wm Dunkyn.
The last of Octob. bapt. Alice Harpe.
The 4th daie of Novēbe. was baptized Tennaker the sonne of John Tennaker.

The xth of November were baptized John & Stepan Throwly the sonnes of Thomas Throwlye.

The xixth of Novĕb. was bapt. Susan Shrobsell the Daught. of Rychard Shroubsol.

The 22th of Nouĕber was baptized Ann Place the Daughter of William Place.

The 6th of Januarie was baptized John Juce the sonne of Richard Juce.

The 23th of Januarie was bapt. John Bassock.

The same daie was baptized Thomas Pettyt sonne of Cirriack Pettyt, Esquire.

The first daie of ffeb was bapt^d Alice Goddard.

The 3^d of March was baptized Edward Kyng the sonne of Thomas Kyng.

The xvth of March was bapt^d Alice Bocher the daughter of Phyllypp Boucher.

Here entreth the yere of our Lord 1564.

The 16th of Aprill was bap^d Florence Jacob the Daught^r of Mathew Jacob.

The 20th daie of Aprill was bapt. Richard Paramour the sonne of Wiłłm Paramour.

The 24 of Maie was bapt^d Richard Howesse.

The 18th of June was bapt^d Wiłłm Spencer.

WILLIAM PLACE,
RICHARD RUCK,
THOMAS HENDMAN. ⊕

Page 4.

The 23th of June was bapt^d Rychard Adie.

The 3^d daie of Septĕb. was baptized Joan Clifford the Daught^r of Robt. Clifford.

The xth of Septĕb. was baptized Thomas Presson the sonne of Rychard Presson.

The 8th of Octob was baptized Georg Jefferye the sonne of Water Jefferye.

The 19th of Octob^r was Baptized Robt Porredge the sonne of Stephan Porredge.

The iij^d of December was Baptized Susan Carr the Daughter of James Carr.

The ixth of Januarie was baptized Elizabethe Throwley the daught. of Tho. Throwley.

The 24th of Januarie was bapt. Barbara Best the Daughter of John Best.

The 28th of Januarie was baptized Marie Haworth the daughter of . . · Haworth.

The 23th of ffeb was bapt^d Thomas Bocher the sonne of Philypp Bocher.

The 6th of March was baptized Edmund Golson the sonne of John Golson.

Here entreth the yere of our Lord 1565.

The xiijth of Aprill was bapt. Christopher Paramour the sonne of Wm Paramour.

The xviijth of June was bapt^d Edward Laurence the sonne of Wiłłm Laurence.

The xxijth of June was bapt^d Joan Jacob daughter of Mathew Jacob.

The iiij of Julye was bapt^d Alice Hanning the daughter of Nicholas Hanninge.

The 8th of Julye was bapt^d Arthure Rucke the sonne of Wiłłm Rucke.

The xixth of Julye was bapt^d Barbara Cowp the Daughter of John Cowpe.

The xxixth of Julye was bapt^d Rose Shroubsoll the Daughter of Christop^s Shroubsoll.

The iij^d of August was bapt^d Tomsyn Hammon the daughter of Richard Hammon.

The xijth of August was bapt^d Rychard Cornish the sonne of Philipp Cornishe.

The last of August was bapt^d Alice Mann the daughter of Laurence Man.

The second of Septēb. was bapt^d Hammon Shroubsoll the sonne of Richard Shroubsoll.

The viijth of Septēb. was baptized Margaret Carter ye daughter of Richard Carter.

The xiiijth of Septēb. was bapt^d Edward Blanket the sonne of Thomas Blankett.

The xvth of Septr was bapt^d Ann Juce the daughter of Wm Juce.

The 16th of Septēb. was bapt. James Tennaker the sonne of John Tennaker.

The first of October was bapt^d Myldred Tylman the daughter of Christoph^s Tylman.

The xxjth of October was bapt^d Rychard Norman, the sonne of Stephan Norman.

The 7th of Nouēb. was bapt. Henrie Juce ye sonne of Richard Juce.

WILLIAM PLACE.
RICHARD RUCK. +
THOMAS HENDMAN. ⊕

Page 5.

The xith of Nouēh. was bapt. Henrie Joan the sonne of Davye Johans.

The xxvth of Nouēb. was bapt. Joan Songer.

The 21th of December was bapt. Thomas Hammon the sonne of Edward Hammon.

The xxvth of Januarie was bapt. Alice Place the daughter of Wiłłm Place.

The vth of ffeb was bapt. Judythe Ley the daughter of Anthoney Leye.

The xxiiij of ffeb was bapt. Margaret Denstone the daughter of Christop⁸ Denstone.

The 8ᵗʰ of March was baptᵈ Edward Collens the sonne of John Collens.

Here entrethe the yere of our Lord 1566.

The third of Aprill was bapt. Margerie Spencer the Daughtʳ of John Spencer.

The xxvᵗʰ of Aprill was baptᵈ Margerie Sharpe the Daughtʳ of Edmond Sharpe.

The xvᵗʰ of June was bapt. John Paramour the sonne of Wiłłm Paramour.

The iiij of Julye was baptᵈ Arthure Porredg the sonne of Stephan Porredge.

The 8ᵗʰ of Julye was baptᵈ Elizabethe Brodstrete the daughtʳ of Edw : Brodstrete.

The 27ᵗʰ of Julye was baptᵈ John Pope the sonne of Thomas Pope.

The 6ᵗʰ of Septeb. was bapt. Margaret Kyng the Daughtʳ of Thomas Kynge.

The 8ᵗʰ of Septeb. was baptᵈ Rose Allen the Daughter of Roger Allen.

The 20ᵗʰ of Septebʳ was baptᵈ Thomas Golson the sonne of John Golson.

The 11ᵗʰ of October was baptᵈ Alyce Shroubsoll the Daughtʳ of Rychard Shroubsoll.

The 27ᵗʰ of Octobʳ was baptᵈ Wiłłm Goddard the sonne of George Goddard.

The 8ᵗʰ of Nouebʳ was baptᵈ Marie Donkyne.

The xiᵗʰ of Jan. was baptᵈ Ellionor Place.

The ix of March was baptᵈ Joan Roger.

Here entreth the yere of our Lord 1567.

The xxviᵗʰ of March was baptᵈ Joan Souger the Daughter of Edward Songer.

The 6ᵗʰ of Aprill was baptᵈ John ffryar.

The 6ᵗʰ of Julye was baptᵈ Catharine Throwley the Daughtʳ of Thomas Throwley.

The 30ᵗʰ of July was baptᵈ Tomsyn Tennaker.

The xᵗʰ of August was baptᵈ Joan Presson.

The 27ᵗʰ of August baptᵈ Thomas Shroubsoll.

The 5ᵗʰ of Octobʳ was baptized John Brodstrete the sonne of Edward Brodstreet.

The xvᵗʰ of Octobʳ was baptᵈ Susan Jacob the Daughter of Mathew acob.

The ſame day was baptᵈ Edward Maxsted the sonne of Wylliam Maxsted.

WILLIAM PLACE.
RYCHARD RUCK.
THO. HENDMAN. ⊕

Page 6.

The 27ᵗʰ of October was baptᵈ Henrie Penystone the sonne of . . . Penystone.

The first of Nouēbʳ was baptᵈ Thomas Clyfford.

The 9ᵗʰ of Nouēbʳ baptᵈ Tho : Juce.

The 26ᵗʰ of Nouēbʳ was baptᵈ Ann Hãmon.

The 30ᵗʰ of Nouēber was bapt. Ann Howesse.

The ixᵗʰ of Januarie was baptᵈ John Place the sonne of Ralf Place.

The first of ffeƀ was bapt. Rychard Jefferye.

The 8ᵗʰ of ffeƀ was baptᵈ Elizabeth Porredge.

The xxixᵗʰ of ffeb was baptᵈ Davyd Metcaufe.

The 8ᵗʰ of March was bapt. Christopʳ Haukes.

The same Day was baptᵈ Edward Paramour.

The 14ᵗʰ of March was baptᵈ John Carr.

The same Day was baptᵈ Margaret Spencer.

The 21ᵗʰ of March were bapt. Roƀt & Elizabeth Joans.

The 22ᵗʰ of March was bapt. Joan Shroubsoll.

Here entrethe the yere of our Lord 1568.

The 28ᵗʰ of March was baptᵈ William Pettyt.

The 18ᵗʰ of Aprill was baptᵈ Edward Norman the sonne of Stephan Norman.

The 28ᵗʰ of Aprill was baptᵈ Dennys Hallowaye.

The 20ᵗʰ of June was baptᵈ Stephan Blunkett the sonne of Thomas Blunkett.

The xiᵗʰ of Julye was baptᵈ Margaret Wills.

The last of Julye was baptᵈ Willm ffoller.

The xiijᵗʰ of August was baptᵈ Tomsin Halin.

The 24ᵗʰ of Octoƀʳ was bapt. John Golson.

The first of Nouēbʳ waa baptᵈ Rychard Gylbert.

The 7ᵗʰ of Nouēbʳ was bapt. Ann Bruke.

The 24ᵗʰ of Nouēbʳ was bapt. John Balden.

The 28ᵗʰ of Nouēbʳ was baptᵈ Elizabeth Pope.

The vᵗʰ of Decēber was baptᵈ Wᵐ Whetstone.

The 6ᵗʰ of ffeƀ was baptᵈ Mathias Woodwall.

The 26ᵗʰ of ffeƀ was baptᵈ Edward Shroubsoll.

The xiᵗʰ of March was baptᵈ Margaret Pecknam.

The 16ᵗʰ of March was baptᵈ Bennet Braer.

Here entreth the yere of our Lord 1569.

The xviij of May was baptᵈ John Shroubsoll.

The 29ᵗʰ of Octoƀ was baptᵈ Willm. Littlewood.

The xviij of Decēbʳ was baptᵈ Ann Denslake.

The xij Jauuareᵉ was baptᵈ Margeᵉ Porredg.

The xvᵗʰ of Jan. was baptᵈ John Spencer.

The same Daie was baptᵈ Susan Balden.

The 24ᵗʰ ffeƀ was baptᵈ Dorothie Dylett.

The xiiᵗʰ of March was baptᵈ John Shroubsoll.

Here Entreth the yere of our Lord 1570.

The 31th of March was bapt^d Elizab : Blankett.
The 20th of Aprill was bapt^d John Throwley.
The 16th of May was bapt^d Ann Jacob.
The iiij of June was bapt. Tho : Roger.
The 16th of June was bapt. Elizabeth Haukes.
The xxvth of June was bapt. Alice Cooper.
The iiijth of August was bapt^d Edmond Ellis.
The 6th of August was bapt. William Juce.
The xvth of Septēb^r was bapt. Mary Howesse.
The xvijth of Septeb. was bapt. Willm. Smyth.
[*blank*] of Nouēb. was bapt. Ann Norman.

WILLIAM PLACE.
RYCHARD RUCK.
THOMAS HENDMAN. ⊕

Page 7.

The xth of Nouēb^r was bapt^d Rabish Hãmon.
The xith of Nouēb^r was bapt^d John Tennaker.
The 4th of Decēb^r was bapt^d John Golson.
The 21th of Decēber was bapt. Elizab. Gilbert.
The 24th of Decēber was bapt. Thomas Whetstone.
The 25th of Decēb^r were bapt. Tho : & Marg^y Dunkyn.
The ixth of Januarie was bapt. Avis Paramour.

This is the end of the old register, all the Christennings from the ixth of Januarie 1570 to the xxiijth of Nouember [1571] ar wantinge, and ar not to be found in any of our church bookes.

———

Here entreth the yere of our Lord 1571.

The xxiijth of Nouēber was bapt^d John Maxsted.
The sixt of Januarie was bapt^d John Tennaker.
The xth of Jan. was bapt^d John Woodwall.
The xxth of ffeb was bapt^d Anthonie Oliver.
The xxixth of feb. was bapt^d Tho : Bradford.
The xiijth of March was bapt^d Thomas Rucke.

Here entreth the yere of our Lord 1572.

The 4th of Aprill was bapt. Susan Johnson.
The 7th of May was bapt. Stephan Paramor.
The ixth of May was bapt. Ann Wantforthe.
The 23th of May was bapt. Mathew Allen.
The 8th of June was bapt^d Thomas Spencer.
The xth of Septeb^r was bapt. Songar Throwley.
The xijth of Septeb^r was bapt^d Elyn Bratt.
The xth of Octob^r was bapt^d John Lye.

Hitherto the names ar exhibited to yᵉ ordinarie.

The xxjᵗʰ of Nouẽbʳ was bapt. Margaret Juce Daughtʳ of Richard Juce.
The xxiijᵗʰ of Nouẽbʳ was baptized Mathew Balden the sonne of John Balden.
The xxxᵗʰ of Nouẽbʳ was baptᵈ Andrew Dilett.
The iiijᵗʰ of Januarie was baptᵈ Joan Watts.
The 25ᵗʰ of Jan. was baptᵈ Tomsyn Bartlett.
The 8ᵗʰ of feẞ was bapt. Catharine Hãmon.
The xvᵗʰ of feẞ was bapt. Anne Penystone.
The 21ᵗʰ of ffeẞ was bapt. Christopʳ Shroubsoll.
The xvᵗʰ of March was bapt. Joan Cocke.
The 21ᵗᵇ of March was bapt. Edmund Roger.

Here entreth the yere of our Lord 1573.

The 19ᵗʰ of Aprill was baptᵈ Willm Norman.
The 22ᵗʰ of May was baptᵈ Margaret Tennaker.
The 25ᵗʰ of July was bapt. Mathew Clyfford.
The 30ᵗʰ of August was bapt. Joan Golson.
The 20ᵗʰ of Septeʳ was bapt. Ann Smyth.
The 21ᵗʰ of October was bapt. Priscilla Jacob.
The xiᵗʰ of Nouẽbʳ was bapt. Susan Broadstreet.
The xxijᵗʰ of Nouẽbʳ was bapt. Martha Jefferye.
The xxvᵗᵇ of Nouẽbʳ was bapt. Thomas Poredge.
The ixᵗʰ of Decẽbʳ was baptᵈ Amos Abram.
The 26ᵗʰ of December was baptᵈ Mathew Spencer.
The xxviijᵗʰ of Januarie was bapt. John Cocke.
The 22ᵗʰ of feẞ was baptᵈ Avis Grimsell.

WILLIAM PLACE.
RICHARD RUCK.
THOMAS HENDMAN. ⊕

Page 8.

thus far yᵉ names ar exhibited to yᵉ Ordinarie.

Here entreth the yere of our Lord 1574.

The 2ᵈ of May was baptᵈ Robᵗ Maxsted.
The ixᵗʰ of May was baptᵈ Jonas Howesse.
The 6ᵗʰ of June was baptᵈ Margaret Maxsted.
The xxᵗʰ of June was baptᵈ Richard Blankett.
The first of August was bapt. John Page the sonne of Margaret Page basborne.
The xvᵗʰ of August was baptᵈ Henrie Coossen.
The xvᵗʰ of Septeẞʳ was baptᵈ John Goodden.
The first of October was baptᵈ Abrahã Bradford.
The 8ᵗʰ of Decẽbʳ was baptᵈ Stephan Allyn the sonne of Nicholas Allyn.
The 28ᵗʰ of Decẽbʳ was baptᵈ Tomsyn Woodwall.
The iijᵈ of ffeẞ was baptᵈ Mathew Spencer, the sonne of John Spencer.

The sixt of March was bapt^d Alice Mills the Daughter of John Mills.
The xij of March was bapt^d Mathew Pope the sonne of Thomas Pope.
The xxth of March was bapt. John Pollard the sonne of Edward Pollard.

Here entreth the yere of our Lord 1575.

The xth of Aprill was bapt^d Marion Brooke the Daughter of William Brooke.
The 28th of Aprill was bapt^d William Husseye the sonne of John Hussey.
The 8th of May was bapt. John Chillenden the sonne of Willm. Chillenden.
The 22th of June was bapt. Raynold Shroubsoll the sonne of Richard Shroubsoll the young^r.
The 20th of Julye was bapt. Thomas Haukyns the sonne of Thomas Haukyns the younger.
The 26th of August was bapt. John Cornish the sonne of Barbara Cornishe, Base borne.
The 28th of Septēb^r was bapt. Thomas Shroubsoll the sonne of Nicholas Shroubsoll.
The same daie was bapt. John Breet the sonne of Nicholas Breet.
The xxixth of Octob^r was bapt^d Marie Shroubsoll the Daughter of Robert Shroubsoll.
The 21th of Nouēb^r was bapt. Michaell Dylett the sonne of Simon Dilett.
The 22th of Decēber was bapt. William Grimsell the sonne of Stephan Grimsell.
The 26th of Decēb^r was bapt. Georg Rucke the sonne of William Rucke.
The 6th ffeb was bapt. Ann Rogers the Daughter of John Rogers.
The xith of feb was bapt^d John Jacob the sonne of Mathew Jacob.
The xxiijth of feb was bapt. Wylliam Tennaker the sonne of John Tennaker.
The xxvith of feb was bapt. Ann Brewer the Daught^r of Thomas Brewer.
The xviijth of March was bapt. Laurence Bucke the sonne of Paule Bucke.
The same Daie was bapt. Bennet Dine the Daughter of Edward Dine.
The 21th of March was bapt. Ann Raynold.

WILLIAM PLACE.
RICHARD RUCK.
THOMAS HENDMAN. ⊕

Page 9.

Here entreth the yere of our Lord 1576.

The 8th of Aprill was bapt^d Joan Norman the the Daughter of Stephan Norman.
The xixth of June was bapt^d Avis Allen the Daughter of Christopher Allen.
The 27th of Julye were bapt. Raynold & ffaythe sonne & Daughter of Edward Sythe.

The 29 of July was bapt^d Marie Haukyns the Daughter of Thomas Haukyns.

The 23^{the} of Septēb^r was christened Thomas Balden the sonne of John Balden.

The same daye was bapt. Tomsyu Pecknam the Daughter of Marke Pecknam.

The 7th of Octob^r was bapt. Alice Blankett the Daughter of William Blanket.

The xiiij of of Octob^r was bapt. Sara Jefferye the Daughter of Water Jefferye.

The xith of Noueb^r was bapt. Edmund Raynolds the sonne of John Raynolds.

The xiij of Januar. was bapt^d Wiłłm Bradford the sonne of John Bradford.

The vth of Decēb^r was bapt^d Joan Throweley the Daughter of Thomas Throwley.

The 20th of Januarie was bapt. John Gooddyn the sonne of John Gooddyn.

The 27th of feb was bapt. Marie Ore the Daughter of Andrewe Ore.

The first of March were bapt. Edward & Stephan Pope the sonnes of Thomas Pope.

The xvth of March was bapt. Joan Brodstreet the Daught^r of Edw : Brodstreete.

Here entrethe the yere of our Lord 1577.

The 4th of Aprill was bapt. Thomas Chillenden the sonne of John Chillenden.

The 8th of Aprill was bapt. Ann Shroubsoll the Daughter of Rychard Shroubsoll.

The 18th of Aprill was bapt. Issabell Presson the Daughter of William Presson.

The 22th of May was bapt. . . . . Hussey the Daughter of John Hussey.

The 16th of May was bapt. Cirriack Ellis the sonne of John Ellis.

The 16th of June was bapt. Rychard Bucke the sonne of Henrie Bucke.

The 28th of Julye was bapt. Alice Chillenden the Daughter of William Chillenden.

The 20th of Septēb^r was bapt. Elizabeth Maxsted the Daughter of Rychard Maxsted.

The 22th of Septēb^r was bapt. Joan Pollard the Daughter of Edward Pollard.

The 29th of Septēb^r was bapt. John Cosen the sonne of John Cosen.

The 8th of Octob^r was bapt. Henrie Haukyns the sonne of Thomas Haukyns the younger.

The 24th of Nouēb^r was bapt. Marie Wetherling.

Thus far certified the 16th of . . . to the . . .

WILLIAM PLACE,
RICHARD RUCKE,
THOMAS HENDMAN. ⊕

Page 10.

The 23th of Decembr was bapt. Theophily Spencer the sonne of John Spencer.

The 29th of Januarie was baptd John Bucke the sonne of Paule Bucke.

The xxiith of feb was bapt. Avis Raynolds the Daughter of Christopher Raynolds.

The 14th of March was baptd Ann Rucke the Daughter of Wiłłm Rucke.

Here entreth the year of our L. 1578.

The 31th of March was bapt. Dorythye Pettyt the Daughter of Henrie Pettyt.

The same Daie was bapt. John Raynold the sonne of John Raynold.

The 20th of Aprill was bapt. Dennis Maxsted the Daughter of John Maxsted.

The 25th of Aprill was bapt. Marke Greene the sonne of Thomas Greene.

The 27th of Aprill was bapt. Jane Tennaker the Daughter of John Tennaker.

The first of June was bapt. Alice Roger the Daughter of John Roger.

The 25th of June was bapt. Susan Maxsted the Daughter of Raynold Maxsted.

The 24th of Julye was bapt. Joan Brett.

The 6th of Julye was bapt. Michaell Bassett the sonne of Albert Bassett.

The 23th of Julye was bapt. Edward Raynold the sonne of Henrie Raynold.

The 27th of Julye was bapt. Ellenor Abram the daughter of Raynold Abram.

The same day was bapt. Margaret Grimsell the Daughter of Stephan Grimsell.

The 20th of August was bapt. Christopher Jacob the sonne of Mathie Jacob.

The same Daie was bapt. Elizabeth Brooke the Daughter of Wiłłm Brooke.

The 5th of Octõbr was bapt. Isaac Chillenden the sonne of Wiłłm Chillenden.

The same Daie was bapt. John Hussey the sonne of John Hussey.

The xixth of Octobr was bapt. Martha Perkyn the Daughter of Rychard Perkyn.

The 29th of Octobr was bapt. Dennis Shroubsoll, the Daughter of Nicholas Shroubsoll.

The 9th of Nouẽbr was bapt. Sara Woodwall the Daughter of John Woodwall.

The 22th of Nouẽber was bapt. Willyam Blankett the sonne of Wiłłm Blankett.

The 7th of Decẽbr was bapt. Ann floid the Daughter of Davye ffloid.

The 24ᵗʰ of Decēbʳ was baptᵈ Ralf Chillenden the sonne of John Chillenden.

The 27ᵗʰ of Decēbʳ was bapt. Joan Bucke the Daughter of James Bucke.

The 28ᵗʰ of Decēbʳ was bapt. Wiłłm Bushe the sonne of Wiłłm Bushe.

The 2ᵈ of ffeb. was bapt. Edward Shroubsell the son of Rychard Shroubsoll the youngʳ.

WILLIAM PLACE,
RICHARD RUCK,
THOMAS HENDMAN. ⊕

Page 11.

The second of feb was bapt. Marke Croyden the sonne of Andrew Croyden.

The 15ᵗʰ of feb was bapt. Mathew Norman the sonne of Stephan Norman.

Here entreth the yere of our Lord 1579.

The 25ᵗʰ of March was bapt. Barbara Napleton the Daughter of Jacob Napleton.

The 5ᵗʰ of Aprill was bapt. Danyell Haukyns the sonne of Thomas Haukyns the yaunger.

The 20ᵗʰ of Aprill was baptᵈ Jane Shroubsoll the Daughter of Robert Shroubsoll.

The 10ᵗʰ of May was bapt. Thomas Dine the sonne of Edward Dine.

The same Day was bapt Luce Jefferye the Daughter of Water Jefferye.

The 24ᵗʰ of May was bapt. Troth Balden the Daughter of John Balden.

The 21ᵗʰ of June was bapt. Rychard Scott the sonne of Elizabeth Scot baseborne.

The 2ᵈ of August was bapt. Elizabeth Smyth the Daughter of Edward Smyth.

The 9ᵗʰ of August was bapt. Avis Rayner the Daughter of Samuell Rayner.

The 23ᵗʰ of August was bapt. Thomas Ore the sonne of Andrew Ore.

The 30ᵗʰ of August was bapt. Marie Pettyt the Daughter of Henrie Pettyt, gent.

The 6ᵗʰ of Septēbʳ was bapt. Ann Bucke the Daughter of Henrie Bucke.

The 18ᵗʰ of Octob was bapt. Wiłłm Shroubsoll the sonne of John Shroubsoll.

The 20ᵗʰ of Nouēhʳ was bapt. John Abram the sonne of Raynold Abram.

The 6ᵗʰ of Decēbʳ was bapt. Venicome Goodden the sonne of John Goodden.

The 20ᵗʰ of Decēbʳ was bapt. Adam Spencer the sonne of John Spencer.

The 20th of Januarie was bapt. Ann Bayley the Daughter of John Bayley.

The same Day was bapt. Jane Pope the Daughter of Thomas Pope.

The 27th of Januarie was bapt. Rychard Bradford the sonne of John Bradford.

The 28th of feb was baptd John Rucke the sonne of Wiłłm Rucke.

The 13th of March was bapt. Thomas Ryder the sonne of Danyell Rider.

Here entreth the yere of our Lord 1580.

The 17th of Aprill was bapt. Ann Bucke the Daughter of Paule Bucke.

The first of May was bapt. Mathie Carter the sonne of John Carter.

The same Daie were bapt. John & Abraham the sonnes of ffrances Scott.

WILLIAM PLACE.

RICHARD RUCK.

THOMAS HENDMAN. ⊕

Page 12.

The 18th of Maie was bapt. Elizabeth Maxsted the Daughter of Raynold Maxsted.

The 23th of May was bapt. Elizabeth Masters a stranger.

The 27th of Julie was bapt. Marie Hills the Daughter of Hercules Hills.

The 24th of August was bapt. Michaell Jacob the sonne of Mathie Jacob.

The 24th of August was bapt. Sara Raynolds the Daughter of Christopher Raynolds.

The 28th of August was bapt. Christopher Bucke the sonne of James Bucke.

The 4th of Septebr was bapt. Dennis Maxsted the Daughter of Rychard Maxsted.

The vith of Septebr was bapt. Susan Haukins the Daughter of Thomas Haukyns the youngr.

The i8th of Septebr was bapt. Edward Rucke the son of Adam Rucke.

The 21th of Septebr was bapt. Susan Hussey the Daughter of John Hussey.

The 28th of Septebr was bapt. Margaret Cosen the Daughter of John Cosen.

The 2d of Octobr was bapt. Ann Pyrkym the Daughter of Rychard Pyrkyn.

The 9th of Octobr was bapt. Parnell Pollard the Daughter of Edward Pollard.

The 26th of Octobr was bapt. Moses Napleton the sonne of Jacob Napleton.

Thus far certified the 19th of Octobr 1580.

The 30th of Octobr was bapt. Ellenor Shroubsoll the Daughter of Robt Shroubsoll.

The 13th of Nouēb^r was bapt. Joan Shroubsoll the Daughter of Rychard Shroubsoll.

The 27th of Nouemb^r was bapt. Margarett Chillenden the Daughter of John Chillenden.

The 26th of Decēb^r was bapt^d Joan Dine the Daught^r of Edward Dine.

The 8th of Januarie was bapt^d Joan Tennaker the Daughter of John Tennaker.

The 7th of feb was bapt. Cirriacke Pettyt the sonne of Henrie Pettyt gent.

The xixth of feb was bapt. Hammon Shroubsoll the sonne of Nicholas Shroubsoll.

The same daie was bapt^d Willm flud the sonne of Davie flod.

The 11th of March was bapt. Issabell Blanket the Daughter of William Blanket.

The 16th of March was bapt. Susan Basset the daughter of Susan Basset.

Here entreth the yere of our Lord 1581.

The 23th of Aprill was bapt. Rychard Shroubsoll the sonne of Rychard Shroubsoll.

The same Daye was bapt^d Elizabeth Chillenden the daughter of William Chillenden.

The 24th of May was bapt^d Tomsyn Grimsell the Daughter of Stephan Grimsell.

The 4th of June was bapt. Alice Raynolds the Daughter of John Raynolds.

The 21th of June were bapt^d Thomas & Willm the sonnes of Thomas Keler.

The same Day was bapt^d Susan the Daughter of Willm Rucke.

WILLIAM PLACE.
RICHARD RUCKE.
THOMAS HENDMAN. ⊕

Page 13.

The xviij of June was bapt Christopher Bradford the sonne of John Bradford.

The 25th of June was bapt. Nicholas Roger the sone of John Roger.

The 8th of Julye was bapt. Catharine Bushe the Daughter of Willm Bushe.

Thus far certified the 24th of Julye.

The 5th of August was (Joan *crossed out*) Catheron Bayley the Daughter of John Bayley.

The first of Octob^r was bapt. Avis Balden the Daughter of John Balden.

The same Day was bapt. Henrie Bucke the sonne of Peter Bucke.

The 28th of Decēb^r was bapt. Rychard Haukyns the sonne of Thomas Haukyns, Ju., gent.

The 11th of feb were bapt. Thomas & Dorothie the children of Thomas Throwley.

The 18th of feb was bapt. Rychard the sonne of Nicholas Handley.
The same Daie was bapt. Margaret Ore the Daughter of Andrew Ore.
The 25th of feb were bapt. Mathie & Susan the children of Nicholas Brett.
The 4th of March was bapt. Elizabeth Woodwall the Daughter of John Woodwall.
The 11th of March was bapt. Margaret Carter the Daughter of John Carter.

Here entreth the yere of our Lord 1582.

The 8th of Aprill was bapt. Willm Harris the sonne of Davye Harris.
The 19th of Aprill was bapt. Otnell Perkyn the sonne of Rychard Perkyn.
The same Daie was bapt. John Smyth the sonne of Edward Smyth.
The 6th of May was bapt. John Rayner the son of Samuell Rayner.
The 17th of June was bapt. Daniell Rucke the sonne of Adam Rucke.
The same Day was bapt. Christopher Pope the sonne of Thomas Pope.
The same Day was bapt. Valentine Rider the sonne of Danyell Rider.
The first of Julye was bapt. Abraham Spencer the sonne of John Spencer.

Thus far certified the 5th of August.

The 22th of August was bapt. Willm Shroubsoll the sonne of Willm Shroubsoll.
The 26th of August was bapt. Martha Heler the Daughter of Mathew Heler.
The 2^d of Septēb^r was bapt. Samuell Maxsted the sonne of Raynold Maxsted.
The last of Septēb^r was bapt. Thomas Buck the sonne of Paule Bucke.
The same Daie was bapt. Austen Hills the sonne of Hercules Hills.
The 21th of Octōb. was bapt. Rychard Hesell the sonne of Rychard Hesell.
The 25th of Octōb^r was bapt. Henrie Pettyt the sonne of Henrie Pettyt, gent.
The 26th of Decemb was bapt. John Browne the sonne of John Browne.

WILLIAM PLACE,
RICHARD RUCK,
THOMAS HENDMAN. ⊕

Page 14.

The 28th of December was bapt. Joan Shroubsoll the daughter of Robt Shroubsoll.
The 13th of Januarie was bapt. Joan Keler the Daughter of Thomas Keler.

C

The 20ᵗʰ of Januarie was bapt. Ann Legate the Daughter of John Legatt.

The 27ᵗʰ of Januarie was bapt. Wiłłm Carr the sonne of James Carr.

The 3ᵈ of feƀ was bapt. Susan Chillenden the Daughter of John Chillenden.

The 10ᵗʰ of March was bapt. Roƀt Maxsted the sonne of Rychard Maxsted.

The same Daie was bapt. Ciriack Raynolds the sonne of Christopher Raynolds.

The 24ᵗʰ of March was bapt. . . . Shroubsoll the . . . of Nicholas Shroubsoll.

1583.   Here entreth the yere of our L. 1583.

The 25ᵗʰ of March was bapt. Marie Hussye the Daughter of John Hussye.

The same Daie was bapt. Marie Dine the Daughter of Edward Dine.

The last of March was bapt. Mydrach Gyles the sonne of Robt Gyles.

The 24ᵗʰ of Aprill was bapt. Wiłłm Napleton the sonne of Jacob Napleton.

The same Daie was bapt. Edward Juce the sonne of Nicholas Juce.

The same Daie was bapt. James Bucke the sonne of James Bucke.

The 25ᵗʰ of Aprill was bapt. Henrie Dylet the sonne of Symon Dylett.

The 5ᵗʰ of May was bapt. Thomsyn Cosen the Daughter of John Cosen.

The 12ᵗʰ of May was bapt. Sara Blanket the Daughter of Wylliam Blanket.

The 16ᵗʰ of June was bapt. Priscilla Haukins the Daughter of Thomas Haukyns, gent.

The 30ᵗʰ of June was bapt. Peter Raynold the sonne of John Raynold.

The 25ᵗʰ of Julye was bapt. Thomas Goodden the sonne of John Goodden.

The same Day was bapt. Margaret Rucke the Daughter of Wiłłm Rucke.

The 21ᵗʰ of August was bapt. Mathew Abram the sonne of Raynold Abram.

The same Day was bapt. . . . the Daughter of Davye floid.

The first of Septēbʳ was bapt. William Wingfield the sonne of Wiłłm Wingfield.

The same Day was bapt. Alice Basset the Daughter of Albert Basset.

The 8ᵗʰ of Septembʳ was baptᵈ Edward Watson the sonne of Hammon Watson.

The 15ᵗʰ of Septēbʳ was bapt. Thomas Hanington the sonne of Nicholas Hannington.

The same Daie was bapt. Martha Shroubsoll the Daughter of Rychard Shroubsoll.

The 29th of Septēb^r was bapt. Susan Bayley the Daughter of John Bayley.

The 13th of Octōb. was bapt. Edmund Scott the sonne of Otnell Scott.

WILLIAM PLACE.
RICHARD RUCKE.
THOMAS HENDMAN. ⊕

Page 15.

The 27th of Nouēb^r was bapt. Edward Pollard the sonne of Edward Pollard.

The 24th of Nouēb^r was bapt. Ann Swan the Daughter of Stephan Swan.

The 8th of Decēb^r was bapt. Ann Bush the Daughter of Wiłłm Bushe.

The 26th of Januar^y was bapt. Gertrud the Daughter of Henrie Pettyt, gent.

The 23th of feb. was bapt. Henrie Jacob the sonne of Mathie Jacob.

The same Daie was bapt. Henrie Throwley the sonne of Thomas Throwleye.

The same Daie were bapt. Robert & Anne the children of Nicholas Handleye.

The first of March was bapt. Michaell Bradford the sonne of John Bradford.

The 8th of March was bapt. Edward Shroubsoll the sonne of John Shroubsoll.

1584.   1584.   1584.   1584.

The 5th of Aprill was bapt. Wiłłm Allen the sonne of Wiłłm Allen.

The 19th of Aprill was bapt. Thomas Shroubsoll the sonne of William Shroubsoll.

The 26th of Aprill was bapt. Tomsyn Spencer the Daughter of John Spencer.

The 7th of June was bapt. Stephan Rucke the sonne of Peter Rucke.

The 5th of Julye was bapt. Ann Grimsell.

The 18th of August was bapt. . . . Jdden.

The 29th of Septēber was bapt. Tomsyu the Daughter of Raynold Maxsted.

The 4th of Octob^r was bapt. Mathie Hawes the sonne of Edward Hawes.

The 29th of Nouēb^r was bapt. Isaac Carter the sonne of John Carter.

The 13th of Decēb^r was bapt. Stephan Keeler the sonne of Thomas Keeler.

The 27th of Januarie was bapt. Ann Chillende the Daughter of John Chillenden.

The 24th of feb was bapt. John Juce the son of Nicholas Juce.

The 28th of feb was bapt. Thomas Rucke the sonne of James Rucke.

The 7th of March was bapt. Ann Robynson the Daughter of Richard Robynson.

The 11th of March was bapt. Hammon Brown the sonne of Thomas Browne.

C²

Here entreth the yere of our L. 1585.

The 4th of Aprill was bapt. Rychard Todd the sonne of Nicholas Todd.

The same Daie was bapt. Christopher Abram the sonne of Raynold Abram.

The 26th of May was bapt. John Chillenden the sonne of Willm Chillenden.

WILLIAM PLACE.
RICHARD RUCK.
THOMAS HENDMAN. ⊕

Page 16.

The same Daie was bapt. John Ore the sonne of Andrewe Ore.

The 13th of June was bapt. Ann Adimer the Daughter of John Adimer.

The 22th of August was bapt. Georg Wingfield the sonne of Willm Wingfield.

The 3[d] of October was bapt. Elizabeth Pettyt the Daughter of Henrie Pettyt.

The same Daie was bapt. Jonas flud the sonne of Davye flud.

The same Daie was bapt. Thomas Rucke the sonne of Adam Rucke.

The 10th of Octob[r] was bapt. Alice Stocwood of Selling.

The 24th of Octob[r] was bapt. Ann Croyden the Daughter of Andrew Croyden.

The same Daie was bapt. Joan Scott the Daughter of Otnell Scott.

The last of Octob[r] was bapt. Edward Rucke the sonne of Will Rucke.

The 26th of Nouēb[r] was bapt. Willm Hills.

The 28th of Nouēb[r] was bapt. John Seterye.

The same Daie was bapt. Rychard Marshall the sonne of Mathew Marshall.

The same Daie was bapt. Thomas Maxsted the sonne of Rychard Maxsted.

The 26th of Decēb[r] was bapt. Nicholas Shroubsoll the sonne of Rychard Shroubsoll.

The 16th of Januarie was bapt. Stephan Sedger the sonne of Philip Sedger.

The same Daie was bapt. Elizabeth Cosen the Daughter of John Cosen.

The 23th of Januarie was bapt. Catherine Rider the Daughter of Danyell Rider.

The 30th of Januarie was bapt. James Bucke the sonne of Peter Bucke.

The 30th of Januarie was bapt. Thomas Harris the sonne of Davye Harris.

The 27th of feb was bapt. Robt Throwley the sonne of Thomas Throwley.

The 13th of March was bapt. Thomas Lewes the sonne of Jeams Lewes.

The 16th of March was bapt. Sanger Watson the sonne of Hammon Watson.

Here entreth the yere of our L. 1586.

The 27th of March was bapt[d] William Hannington the son of Nicholas Hannington.

The 30th of March was bapt. Elizabeth Rucke the Daughter of Cirriack Rucke.

The 27th of Aprill was bapt. Ann Rayner the Daughter of Samuel Rayner.

The 8th of May was bapt. Mark the sonne of Albert Bassett.

The 12th of May was bapt. Thomas Golson the sonne of John Golson.

The 15th of May was bapt. Austen the sonne of James Carr.

The 3[d] of June was bapt. John Edwards the sonne of John Edwards.

WILLIAM PLACE.
RICHARD RUCK.
THO. HENDMAN. ⊕

Page 17.

The 15th of Julye was bapt. Marie Allen the Daughter of Wiłłm Allen.

The 17th of Julye was baptized Hope the Daughter of Misacke Cosen.

The 24th of July was baptiz. Josias the sonne of John Goodden.

The 31th of Julye was bapt. Bennet the Daughter of Thomas Haukins, gent.

The 11th of Septẽb[r] was bapt. Thomas Napleton the sonne of Jacob Napleton.

The 18th of Septẽb[r] was baptiz. Elizabeth Swan the Daughter of Stephan Swan.

The 25th of Septẽber was bapt. Rob[t] Spencer the son of John Spencer.

Certified the 28th of September.

The 2[d] of Octob[r] was bapt. Elizabeth Scott the Daughter of Frances Scott.

The 16th of Octob[r] was bapt. Mathie Wingfield the son of Wiłłm Wingfield.

The 6th of Nouẽb[r] was bapt. Edward Howesse the sonne of Edward Howesse.

The same Daie was bapt. Marion the Daughter of . . . Middleton.

The 11th of Decẽb[r] was bapt. Marie Shroubsoll the Daughter of William Shroubsoll.

The 18th of Decẽb[r] was bapt. Edward Bradford the sonne of John Bradford.

The 29th of Decẽb[r] was bapt. Mathie Scott the sonne of James Scott.

Certified the 12th of Januarie.

The 15th of Januarie was bapt. Ambrose Carter the sonne of Wylliam Carter.

The same Daie was bapt. Edward Grimsell the sonne of Stephan Grimsell.

The 22th of Januarie was bapt. Gabriell Hills the son of Hercules Hills.

The 29th of Januarie was bapt. Margaret Scott the Daughter of Otnell Scott.

The 5th of ffeb was bapt. Christopher Maxsted the sonne of Raynold Maxsted.

The 19th of feb was bapt. Christopher Brown the sonne of Thomas Browne.

The same Daie was bapt. Valentine Swift the sonne of Robt Swift.

The 12th of March was bapt. Ann Juce the Daughter of Nicholas Juce.

The same Daie was bapt. Ursella Shroubsoll the Daughter of Robt Shroubsoll.

Here entreth the yere of our L. 1587.

The 26th of March was bapt. Willm Chillenden the sonne of John Chillenden.

The 3^d of Aprill was bapt. Cirriack Carter the sonne of John Carter.

The 15th of May was bapt. Symon Abram the sonne of Raynold Abram.

The 10th of August was bapt. Marie Adymer the Daughter of John Adymer.

The first of Octob^r was bapt. Elizabeth Chillenden the Daughter of Willm Chillenden.

> WILLIAM PLACE.
> RICHARD RUCK.
> THOMAS HENDMAN. ⊕

Page 18.

The 8th of October was bapt. Alice Goodwin the Daughter of Tho: Goodwyn.

The first of Januarie was bapt. Tomsyn Brooke the Daughter of Laurence Brooke.

The 7th of Januarie was bapt. John Hussey the sonne of John Hussey.

The 24th of Januarie was bapt. Elizabeth Rucke the Daughter of William Rucke.

The 2^d of feb was bapt. Christopher the sonne of Austen Kynge.

The 19th of ffeb was bapt. Avis Throwley the Daughter of Thomas Throwley.

The xth of March was bapt. Ann Pope the Daughter of Thomas Pope.

The 13th of March was bapt. Ann Wingfield the Daughter of Wylliam Wingfield.

Thus far certified to the ordinarie.

Here entreth the yere of our L. 1588.

The 14th of Aprill was bapt. Abraham Tayler the sonne of Thomas Tayler.

The 2^d of June was bapt. John Chillenden the sonne of John Chillenden.

The same Day was baptized a child that was borne at Robert Shroubsoll's named Stephan Bassocke.

The 16th of June was bapt. Ann Downe the Daughtr of Thomas Downe.

The ixth of the same month was baptiz. the childe of a poore vagrant woman.

The 7th of Julye was bapt. Otnell Scott the sonne of Otnell Scott.

The same Daie was bapt. Margaret ffroud the Daughter of Joseph ffroud.

The 7th of Aprill was bapt. Danyell Marshall the sonne of Mathew Marshall.

The 14th of Julye was bapt. Marie Edwards the Daughter of John Edwards.

The xxith of Julye was bapt. Ann Bucke the Daughter of Peter Bucke.

The xxvth of Julye was bapt. Henrie Watson the sonne of Hammon Watson.

The xith of August was bapt. Arthure Whatman the sonne of James Whatman.

The 18th of August were bapt. John & Margaret the children of John Smyth.

The 25th of August was bapt. Mathie Blunket the sonne of John Blunket.

Thus far certified.

The xvth of Septêbr was bapt. Otnell Shroubsoll the sonne of Rychard Shroubsoll.

The 6th of Octobr was bapt. Mathie Hammon the sonne of Edward Hammon.

The same Daie was bapt. Sara Bucke the Daughter of James Bucke.

The xth of Nouêbr was bapt. Ann Shroub. the Daughter of Wyllyam Shroubsoll.

The same Daie was bapt. Margaret Goose the Daughter of Thomas Goose.

The 3d of Nouêbr was bapt. Edward Abram the sonne of Raynold Abram.

WILLIAM PLACE.
RICHARD RUCKE.
THOMAS HENDMAN. ⊕

Page 19.

The 27th of Nouêb was bapt. Susan Shroubsoll the Daughter of Edward Shroubsoll.

The viijth of Decêbr was bapt. . . . Carr the . . . of James Carr.

The 28th of Decêbr was bapt. Willm Andrewes the sonne of Willm Andrewes.

The first of Januarie was bapt. . . . Pantry the . . . of Ralf Pantrye.

The 16th of feb was bapt. Arthure Rucke.

The xxiiijth of feb was bapt. Edward Allen the sonne of . . . Allen.

The 8th of March was bapt. Joan Napleton the Daughter of Jacob Napleton.

The same Daie was bapt. Rychard Swan the sonne of Stephan Swan.

The same Daie was bapt. Catharine Tadd the Daughter of Nicholas Tadd.

The xvth of March was bapt. Thomas Purvyor the sonne of Thomas Purvior.

The same Daie was bapt. Marie Hanington.

The same Daie was bapt. . . . Scot the . . . of Otnell Scott.

The same Daie was bapt. Avis Scott the Daughter of James Scott.

thus far certified.

Here entreth the yere of our L. 1589.

The 8th of Aprill were bapt. Georg. & Wiłłm the sonnes of Nicholas Juce.

The 4th of Maie was bapt. Christopher Golson the sonne of John Golson.

The 11th of Maie was bapt. John Grimsell the sonne of Stephan Grimsell.

The 18th of Maie was bapt. Susan Croyden the Daughter of Andrew Croyden.

The xxth of Julye was bapt. Ann Balden the Daughter of John Balden.

The 27th of July was bapt. Rychard Swift the sonne of Robt Swyft.

The 3^d of August was bapt^d John Carter the sonne of John Carter.

The 27th of Septeb^r was bapt. Markes Kyng the sonne of Austen Kynge.

Thus far certified.

The 26th of Octob^r was bapt. Susan Browne the Daughter of Thomas Browne.

The 21th of Januarie was bapt^d Alyce Sutton the Daughter of John Sutton.

The xith of Januarie was bapt^d James Tennaker the sonne of Edward Tennaker.

The xith of Januarie was bapt^d Jane Rucke the Daughter of Cirriack Rucke.

The 23th of Januarie was bapt. Thomas Brenn the sonne of Thomas Brenn a stranger.

The first of ffeb was bapt. John Spencer the sonne of Stephan Spencer.

WILLIAM PLACE.
RICHARD RUCKE.
THOMAS HENDMAN. ⊕

Page 20.

The 8th of ffeb was bapt. John Downe.

The xvth of feb was bapt. Wiłłm Goose.

The first of March was bapt. Mathew Scott the sonne of Otnell Scott.

The 7th of March was bapt. Wiłłm Rider the sonne of Daniell Rider.

The 22th of March was bapt. Henrie Place the sonne of John Place.

Here entreth the yere of our L. 1590.

The 29th of March was bapt Robt. Shroubsoll the sonne of Wiilm Shroubsoll.

The 5th of Aprill was bapt. Ann ffode the Daughter of . . . ffode.

The xth of Aprill were bapt. Joan and Tomsyn the Daughters of Wm. Rucke.

The 12th of Aprill was bapt. Hercules Hills the sonne of Hercules Hills.

The xxth of Aprill was bapt. fabye the Daughter of John Hussey.

The 20th of May was bapt. Marie Carr the Daughter of James Carr.

The 28th of May was bapt. Ezechiell Maxsted the sonne of Raynold Maxsted.

The 31th of May was bapt. Edward Chillenden the son of John Chillenden.

The 5th of Julye was bapt Catharine Berrye the Daughter of John Berrye.

The —th cf August was baptized Elizabeth Medowe the Daughter of John Medowe.

The 16th of August was bapt. John Maxsted the sonne of Rychard Maxsted.

The 23th of August was bapt. Thomas Brooke the son of Laurence Brooke.

The 30th of August was bapt. Mathew Marshall the sonne of Mathew Marshall.

The 13th of Septēb^r was bapt. Susan Pantry the Daughter of Ralf Pantrye.

The 4th of Octob^r was bapt. Margaret Shroubsoll the Daughter of Edw: Shroubsoll.

Thus far certified the 7th of Octob^r 1590.

The 11th of Octob^r was bapt. Wiilm Abram the sonne of Raynold Abram.

The same Daie was bapt. Priscilla Chappell the Daughter of John Chappell.

The 18th of Octob^r was bapt. Wiilm. Watson the sonne of Hamon Watson.

The same Daie was bapt. Joan Keeler the Daughter of Thomas Keeler.

The 2^d of Nouēb^r was bapt. Gregorie Rand the soñe of Rand.

The 8th of Nouēber was bapt. Elizabeth Bankes the Daughter of James Bankes.

The 2^d of feb was bapt. Catharine Carter the daughter of John Carter.

The 7th of feb was bapt. Robt Sharp the sonne of Robt Sharpe.

The 21th of feb was bapt. Edward Kyng the son of Austen Kyng.

WILLIAM PLACE.
RICHARD RUCKE.
THOMAS HENDMAN. ⊕

Page 21.

The 7th of March was bapt. Elizabeth froud the Daughter of Joseph froud.

The 21th of March was bapt. Wiłłm Edwards the sonne of John Edwards.

Here entreth the yere of o^r L. 1591.

The 11th of Aprill was bapt. John Napleton the sonne of Jacob Napleton.

The 9th of Maie was bapt. Margaret Tennaker the Daughter of Edward Tennaker.

The 12th of June was bapt. Marie Raynold the Daughter of Henrie Raynold.

The 7th of Julie was bapt. Thomas Kyng the sonne of Christopher Kynge.

The 11th of Julie was bapt. Margaret Parke the Daughter of Abraham Parke.

The xijth of Septemb^r was bapt. Ann Ovenden the Daughter of Laurence Ovenden.

Thus far certified xxviijth of October 1591.

The 23th of Octob^r was bapt. Marie Pettit the Daughter of Henrie Pettyt, gent.

The 14th of Nouēb^r was bapt. Wiłłm Travesse the sonne of Edward Travesse.

The 15th of Decemb̃ was bapt. Arthur Whateman the sonne of James Whatman.

The 29th of Decēb. was bapt. Jssabel Rucke the Daughter of Rychard Rucke.

The xvjth of Januarie was bapt. Margaret Purviour the Daughter of Thomas Purvior.

The 30th of Januarie was bapt. Wiłłm Hendman the sonne of Thomas Hendman.

The same Daie was bapt. Joan Browne the Daughter of Thomas Browne.

The 7th of feb̃ was bapt. Marie Cornishe the Daughter of Laurence Cornishe.

The 27th of feb̃ was bapt. Ann Dadson the Daughter of Arthure Dadson.

The 18th of March was bapt. Mathew Norman the sonne of Matthew Norman.

The same Daie was bapt. Thomas Watson the sonne of Hammon Watson.

The same Daie was bapt. Sara Rayner the Daughter of Samuell Rayner.

The 21th of March were bapt. John and Margaret the children of James Scott.

Here entreth yᵉ yere of our L. 1592.

The 27ᵗʰ of March was bapt. Marie Juce the Daughter of Nicholas Juce.

The 2ᵈ of Aprill was bapt. Marie Berry the Daughter of John Berrye.

The 9ᵗʰ of Aprill was bapt. Wiłłm Cornish the sonne of Rychard Cornishe.

The i6ᵗʰ of Aprill was bapt. Alice Chillenden the Daughter of John Chillenden.

The 30ᵗʰ of Aprill was bapt. John Gray the sonne of Robt. Gray.

WILLIAM PLACE.
RICHARD ROCKE.
THOMAS HENDMAN. ⊕

Page 22.

The same Daie was baptᵈ Jean Goose the Daughtʳ of Thomas Goose.

The 9ᵗʰ of Julie was bapt. Nicholas Wood the sonne of Wiłłm Wood.

The 23ᵗʰ of Julie was baptᵈ William Thomas the sonne of John Thomas.

The 30ᵗʰ of Julie was baptᵈ Wiłłm Hills the sonne of Hercules Hills.

The 27ᵗʰ of Septẽbʳ was bapt. Tomsyn the Daughter of Wiłłm Shroubsoll.

The first of Octobʳ was bapt. Robt Bankes the sonne of Jeames Bankes.

The same Daie was baptᵈ John Croyden the sonne of Andrew Croyden.

Thus far certified the 4ᵗʰ of October 1592.

The 8ᵗʰ of October was bapt. James Chappell the sonne of John Chappell.

The 29ᵗʰ of Octob was bapt. Florence Shroubsoll the Daught. of Edw : Shroubsoll.

The 27ᵗʰ of Decẽb. was bapt. Wᵐ Place the sonne of John Place, Jun.

The same Daie was bapt. Susan Tadd the Daughter of Nicholas Tadd.

The 14ᵗʰ of Januarie was bapt. Joan White the Daughter of · · · White.

The 12ᵗʰ of feb was bapt. Joan Lewes the Daughter of James Lewes.

The i8ᵗʰ of feb was baptᵈ Ann Downe the Daughter of Thomas Downe.

The same Daie was baptᵈ Grace Abram the Daughter of Raynold Abram.

The 25ᵗʰ of feb was baptᵈ Marie Meere the Daughter of · · Meere base borne.

The 4ᵗʰ of March was bapt. Elizabeth Bush the Daughtʳ Wᵐ Bushe.

The i6ᵗʰ of March was baptᵈ Anne Keler the Daughter of Thomas Keeler.

The same Daie was bapt^d Susan Rider the Daughter of Daniell Ryder.
The 17th of March were bapt^d Nathaniell & Wiłłm the sonnes of Laurence Brooke.

Here entreth the yere of o^r L. 1593.

The 16th of Aprill was bapt^d Ann Tennaker the Daughter of Edward Tennaker.
The 4th of June was bapt^d Marie Rucke the Daughtèr of Cirriacke Rucke.
The 27th of June was bapt^d Thomas Latt the sonne of John Latt.
The 29th of Julie was bapt^d Henrie Shroubsoll the son of Robt. Shroubsoll.
The 7th of Octob^r was bapt. John Parkes the sonne of Abram Parke.
    Thus far certified the 11th of Octob^r 1593.
                    WILLIAM PLACE.
                    RICHARD RUCKE.
                    THOMAS HENDMAN. ⊕
    Page 23.

The 14th of Octob^r was bapt^d Susan Maxsted the Daughter of Robt. Maxsted.
The same Daie was bapt^d Marie Juce the Daughter of Nicholas Juce.
The same Daie was bapt^d Joan Howesse the Daughter of Rychard Howesse.
The first of Nouëb^r was bapt. Mathewe Balden the sonne of John Balden.
The 4th of Nouëb^r was bapt^d Alice Spencer the Daughter of William Spencer.
The same Daie was bapt^d Grace Kyng the Daughter of Christopher Kynge.
The 25th of Nouëb^r was bapt^d Elizabeth Chappell the Daught^r of John Chappell.
The 6th of Januarie was bapt. Ann Scott the Daughter of James Scott.
The 16th of feb was bapt^d Margerye Gregorie the Daughter Robt. Gregorie.

Here entreth ye yere of o^r L. 1594.

The 14th of Aprill was bapt. John Jdden the sonne of Georg Jdden.
The 21th of Aprill was bapt^d Elizabeth Edwards the Daught^r of John Edwards.
The fourth of August was bapt. William Rucke the sonne of Cirriack Rucke.
The same Daie was bapt^d Marie Rainolds the Daughter of Georg Raynolds.
The 11th of August was bapt. Avis Jacob the Daughter of Cirriack Jacob.
The 29th of Sep^ter was bapt. Elizabeth Wood the Daughter of Wiłłm Wood.
    Thus far certified the 9th of October 1594.

The 20th of Octob^r was bapt^d Thomas Dine the sonne of Edward Dine.

The ioth of Noueb^r was bapt^d Edmund Chillenden the sonne of Wiłłm Chillenden.

The 26th of Decb^r was bapt^d Margerie Shroubsoll the Daughter of Wm Shroubsoll.

The 12th of Januarie was bapt. William Shroubsoll the sonne of Edward Shroubsoll.

The i9th of Januarie was bapt. Marie Travesse the Daught^r of Edward Travesse.

The i9 of feb was bapt^d Ann Whateman the Daughter of James Whateman.

The 16th of feb was bapt^d Rychard Longley the sonne of Edward Longley.   Chauceri (?) luce (?)*

The same Daie was bapt^d Ann Howesse the Daught^r of Rychard Howesse.

The 23 of feb was bapt^d Georg Watson the sonne of Hammon Watson.

The same Daie was bapt^d Elizabeth Shroubsoll the Daughter of Edw : Shroubsoll.

WILLIAM PLACE.
RICHARD RUCKE.
THOMAS HENDMAN. ⊕

Page 24.

The 2^d of March was bapt. Josias Rucke the sonne of Rychard Rucke.

The 6th of March was bapt. Dorothie Best the Daughter of John Best, gent.

Here entreth the yere of our L. i595.

The i3th of Aprill was bapt. Joan Tadd the Daughter of Nicholas Tadd.

The same Daie was bapt. Elizabeth Shroubsoll the Daughter of John Shroubsoll the younger.

The 9th of May was bapt. Edward Tennaker the sonne of Edward Tennaker.

The 25 of May was bapt. Hañion Downe the sonne of Thomas Downe.

The 20th of August was bapt. Ann Kyng ye Daughter of Christopher Kyng.

The same Daie was bapt. Alyce Hills the Daughter of Michaell Hills.

The 27th of August was bapt. Ann Cornish the Daughter of Laurence Cornishe.

The same Daie was bapt^d Jean Maxsted the Daughter of John Maxsted thelder.

The 30th of August was bapt^d Margaret Spencer the Daughter of Wiłłm Spencer.

---

* This infant was buried 22 Feb., and these words apparently have reference to its early death.

The same Daie was bapt^d Elizabeth Juce the Daughter of Stephan Juce.

The 5th of Octob^r was bapt^d ffrances Hills the Daughter of Hercules Hills.

The 9th of Nouẽb^r was bapt^d Sara Thomas the Daughter of John Thomas.

The 23th of Nouẽb^r was bapt^d William Place sonne of William Place, Cler.

The 30th of Nouẽb^r was bapt^d Martha Joanes the Daught^r of Henrie Joanes.

The 28th of Nouẽb^r was bapt. Cirriack Jacob the sonne of Cir. Jacob.

The first of Januarie was bapt^d Elizabeth Lewes the Daughter of James Lewes.

The 9th of feb was bapt. Edward Besant the sonne of Georg Besant.

The 26th of feb was bapt^d Robt. Nox the sonne of John Nox.

The vjth of March was bapt. Edward Okenfold the son of Willm Okenfold.

The 14th of March was bapt^d Tomsyn Raynolds the Daughter of Georg Raynolds.

The xxjth of March was bapt. William Rayner the sonne ·of Samuell Rayner.

The same Daie was bapt^d John Maxsted the sonne of John Maxsted.

The same Daie was bapt. Rychard Goose the sonne of Thomas Goose.

Thus far certified the 2^d of Aprill 1596.

Here entreth the yere of our L. 1596.

The 18th of Aprill was bapt^d Robt. Juce the sonne of Nicholas Juce.

The xxvth of Aprill was bapt^d Nicholas Wood the sonne of William Wood.

The same Daie was bapt^d Margarett Preble the daughter of . . . Preble.

WILLIAM PLACE.
RICHARD RUCKE.
THOMAS HENDMAN. ⊕

Page 25.

The 13th of Maie was bapt^d Dorothie Spencer the Daughter of Thomas Spencer.

The 23th of June was bapt. Edmund Abram the sonne of Raynold Abram.

The 11th of Julie was bapt^d William Tennaker the sonne of Edward Tennaker.

The 29th of August was bapt^d Marie the the Daught^r of . . . Baseborne.

The 12th of Septẽb^r was bapt^d John Shroubsoll the son of Willm Shroubsoll.

The same Daie was bapt^d Tomsyu Spencer the Daughter of Paule Spencer.

Thus far certified the vij^th of Octob^r 1596.

The 24th of October was bapt. Rychard fylcott the son of William ffylcott.

The 3th of Octob^r was bapt^d Avis Marshall the Daughter of Mathew Marshall.

The 7th of Noučb^r was bapt^d James Place the sonne of John Place.

The 24th of Noučb^r was bapt. Cirriack Rucke the son of Cirriack Rucke.

The 7th of Dečeb^r was bapt^d Thomas Howesse the son of Rychard Howesse.

The 12th of Dečeb^r was bapt^d John Raynolds the son of Christopher Raynolds.

The 2^d of Januarie was bapt. Elizabeth Whatman the Daughter of Paule Whatman.

The same Daie was bapt. Stephan Clement the son of Stephan Clement.

The 7th of feb was bapt^d Elizabethe Hempshane the Daughter of Hempshane.

The 23th of Januarie was bapt^d Robert Norman the sonne of Robt. Norman.

The same Daie was bapt^d Thomas Maxsted the sonne of Robt. Maxsted.

The 27th of feb was Bapt^d John Kennard the sonne of John Kennard.

Here entreth the yere of our L. 1597.

The 8th of May was bapt^d John Whatman the son of James Whatman.

The 22th of Maie was bapt^d Elizabethe Pantry the Daughter of Ralf Pantrye.

The 19th of June was bapt^d John Shroubsoll the son of Edward Shroubsoll.

The 3^d of Julie was bapt^d Susan Watson the Daughter of Hamon Watson.

The 7th of August was bapt^d Elizabeth Hills the Daughter of Michaell Hills.

The 14th of August was bapt^d Cirriack Hendman the son of Thomas Hendman.

The 28th of August was bapt^d Sarles Humfry the sonne of Andrew Humfrey.

The 6th of Septěber was bapt^d Water Tompson the sonne of Thomas Tompson.

The 28th of Septěb^r was bapt^d Robt. Moorcroft the sonne of . . . Moorcroft.

WILLIAM PLACE.
RICHARD RUCKE.
THOMAS HENDMAN. ⊕

Page 26.

The 28th of Septemb^r was bapt^d Edward ffylcott the sonne of William ffylcott.

Thus far certified the 11th of Octob^r 1597.

The second of October was bapt^d Georg Besant the sonne of Georg Besant.

The 16th of Octob^r was bapt^d Margaret Jacob the Daughter of Cirriack Jacob.

The 28th of Octob^r was bapt^d Rychard Wood the sonne of William Wood.

The 30th of Octob^r was bapt^d Tomsyn ffroud the Daughter of Joseph ffroud.

The 4th of December was bapt^d Tomsyn Spencer the Daughter of Wiłłm Spencer.

The 26th of Decemb^r was bapt^d Thomas the son of John Shroubsoll the yong^{er}.

Here entreth the yere of o^r L. 1598.

The 26th of March was bapt^d William Badkin the sonne of Rychard Badkyn.

The 16th of Aprill was bapt^d Mathew Adye the sonn of Mathew Adie.

The 23th of Aprill was bapt^d William Pantrye the son of Ralf Pantry.

The 14th of May was bapt^d Henrie Raynolds the son of Georg Raynolds.

The 11th of June was bapt^d Thomas Loue the son of Georg Loue.

The 16th of Julie was bapt^d John Besset the son of Edward Bysset.

The 13th of August was bapt^d Elizabethe Rayner the Daught^r of Samuell Rayner.

The 20th of August was bapt^d Meekenesse Juce the Daught^r of Stephan Juce.

The same Daie was bapt^d Margaret Littlewood the Daught^r of Wiłłm Littlewood.

The 3^d of Septēb^r was bapt^d John Noxe the son of John Nox.

The same Daie was bapt. Thomas Shroubsoll the sonne of Thomas Shroubsoll.

The 23th of September was bapt. Thomas Tompson the son of Thomas Tompson, gent.

The first of Octob^r was bapt. Grace ffylcott the Daught^r of Wiłłm ffylcott.

The same Daie was bapt. Ann Maxsted the daught^r of John Maxsted, Jun.

The 22th of Octob^r was bapt^d Ann Tattersoll the Daught^r of Christ: Tattersoll.

The same day was baptiz. Alice Spencer the Daught^r of Thomas Spencer.

The 19th of Nouemb^r was bapt^d Edw : Thomas son of John Thomas.

The same Daie was Baptz. Elizabeth Shroubsoll the Daught^r of Tho : Shroubsoll.

Wm. Place.

Page 27.

The 26th of Nouēb^r was bapt^d Clement Golson, son of John Golson.

The 10th of Decemb^r was bapt^d Anne Preble Daughter of . . . Preble.

The 17th of Deceb^r was bapt^d Marie Place Daughter of Wm. Place.
The 22th of Januarie was baptized Rychard Snoth son of Miles Snoth.
The iiij of ffeb was baptized Jane Humfray Daught^r of Andrew Hüfray.
The 25th of ffeb. was bapt^d Marie Smythson the Daught^r of . . . Smithson.
The 20th of March was bapt^d Stephan Shroubsoll son of Edward Shoubsoll, med (*sic*).
The same Daie was bapt^d Edward Cornish son of Laurence Cornish.
The same Daie was bapt^d Tomsyn Place daught^r of John Place, sen^r.

Here entreth ye yere of our L. 1599.

The 25th of March was baptized Jonathan Tayler the sonne of Daniell Tayler.
The same Daie was bapt^d John Tennaker the son of Edward Tennaker.
The 15th of Aprill was bapt^d Thomas Norman son of Edward Norman.
The same day was bapt^d Grace Norcote Daught^r of Thomas Norcote.
The 22th of Aprill was bapt^d Margaret Lewes the Daught^r of James Lewes.
The 29th of Aprill was bapt^d Thomas Goose son of Thomas Goose.
The 6th of May was bapt^d Michaell Shroubsoll son of Edward Shroubsoll.
The 13th of May was bapt. Joan Badkyn daught^r of Rychard Badkyn.
The same Daie was bapt^d Joan Shroubsoll Daught^r of John Shroubsoll, Jun.
The 17th of June was bapt. Jonas Parker the sonne of Abram Parker, posthumus.
The same Day was bapt^d Thomas Lawe sonne of Ralf Lawe.
The 24th of June was bapt^d Margerie Packnam Daught^r of Roger Packnam.
The 15th of Julye was bapt. Thomas Wilson son of . . . Wilson.
The same Daie was bapt. Georg Lat son of Thomsyn Late, wid., baseborne.
The 29th of Julye was bapt^d Alice Norman Daught^r of Robt Norman.
The same Daie was bapt^d Marie Enfield daught^r of Wiłłm Enfield.

Wм. Place.

Page 28.
The 26th of August was baptiz. Margaret Giles Daught^r of Marke Giles.
The 9th of Septemb^r was bapt^d Joan Adye the Daught^r of Mathie Adye.
The 16th of Septemb^r was bapt^d Edward Maxsted sonn of Robert Maxsted.
The 30th Day of September was bapt^d . . . Besant the son of Georg Besant.

D

The 2i^th^ of October was bapt^d^ Joan Golson the Daughter of Edmund Golson.

The 25th of Nouemb^r^ was bapt^d^ Wiłłm Wood the son of Wiłłm Wood.

The ix^th^ of December was baptized Joan Shroubsoll the Daught^r^ of Edward Shroubsoll the young^r^.

The xxiij^th^ of December was baptized William Pope son of Mathew Pope.

The 6th of Januar. was bapt^d^ Marie Rucke the daught^r^ of Cirriack Rucke.

The xiij of Januar. was bapt^d^ Edward Shroubsoll the son of William Shroubsoll.

The 27th of Jan. was bapt^d^ Michaell Hills son of Michaell Hills.

The same Daie was bapt^d^ Henrie Nicholas son of Roƀt Nicholas.

The 24th of March was bapt^d^ Elizabeth Lowe Daught^r^ of Georg Lowe.

Here entreth the yere of our Lord 1600   1600.

The sixt of Aprill was baptized Arthur Place son of John Place, Jun.

The 8th day of Aprill was baptized Thomas Downe son of Thomas Downe.

The 20th of Aprill was bapt^d^ Susan Shroubsoll the Daught^r^ of Edward Shroubsoll, med. (*sic*).

The 27th day of Aprill was baptiz. Thomas Juce sonne of Edward Juce.

The 11th of May was bapt^d^ Jaspar Collens son of Edward Collens.

The 18th of May was bapt^d^ Zacharie Preble Daught^r^ of Edw. Preble.

The 28th of May was bapt^d^ Mathew Pryse son of Mathew Prise.

The first of June was bapt^d^ Raynold Maxsted son of John Maxsted, sen.

The 8th of June was bapt^d^ Alice Howesse Daught^r^ of Rychard Howesse.

The 17th of August was baptiz. John Spencer son of William Spencer.

The 7th of Septeb̃^r^ was baptiz^d^ Edward Jacob son of Cir : Jacob.

The same Daie was bapt^d^ Roƀt Golson son of John Golson.

The 28th of Septeb̃^r^ was bapt^d^ James Daie the son of John Daie.

The i9^th^ of Octoƀ^r^ was baptiz. Tomsyn Lewes Daught^r^ of James Lewes.

The same Day was bapt^d^ Elizabeth Maxsted the Daught^r^ of John Maxsted the younger.

WM. PLACE.

Page 29.

The xij^th^ of Nouember was bapt^d^ Rychard Porredge son of Tho. Porredge.

The same Daie was baptiz. John Tattersoll son of Christopher Tattersoll.

The xj^th^ of Januarie was bapt^d^ Joan ffyn Daught^r^ of Edw: ffynñ.

The same Day was bapt^d^ Susan Stenyngs Daught^r^ of Christopher Stenyngs.

The viij^th^ Day of ffeƀ was bapt^d^ Ann Downe Daught^r^ of Edward Downe.

The 16th of ffeb was bapt^d Stephan ffroud son of Joseph ffroud.

The xxiith of ffeb was bapt^d Rychard Shroubsoll son of Tho : Shroubsoll.

The same Day was bapt^d Ann Tayler Daught^r of Danyell Tayler.

The ffirst Day of March was bapt^d John Place son of William Place.

The xiiijth Daie of March was bapt^d Margerie the Daught^r of Barbarow Heeler, wid., a baseborne child.

Certified Aprill the 9th 160i.

Here entreth the yere of our Lord 160i   160i.

The xiij day of Aprill was bapt^d Marie Chappell the Daught^r of John Chappell.

The 27th of Aprill was bapt^d Mathew Ball son of John Ball.

The 7th of June was bapt^d Joan Snoth daught^r of Miles Snoth.

The same Daie was bapt^d John Ball son of Ann Ball, basborne.

The 12th of Julye was bapt^d Ann Pope Daught^r of Mathew Pope.

The second of August was bapt^d Alice Shroubsoll Daught^r of Edward Shroubsoll.

The same Day was bapt^d Thomas Juce son of Stephan Juce.

The 16th of August was bapt^d Alice Travesse daught^r of Edward Travesse.

The 30th of August was bapt^d Susan Norcote daught^r of Thomas Norcote.

The 6th of September was bapt^d Elenor Loue daught^r of Alexander Loue.

The 20th of Septeb^r was bapt^d Elizabeth Shroubsoll daught^r of Edward Shroubsoll.

The 8th of Noueber was bapt^d Edward Collens son of Edward Collens.

The same day was bapt. Elizabeth Spencer daught^r of Thomas Spencer.

The 15th of Nouember was baptiz. John Golson the sonn of Edmund Golson.

The same Day was baptiz. Leonard Thomas son of John Thomas.

The 22th of Nouember was baptiz. Ellenore fylcote daughter of William fylcote.

The 13 of December was baptiz. Christopher Shroubsoll son of Edward Shroubsoll.

The third of Januar. was baptiz. Georg Best son of John Best, gent.

WM. PLACE.

Page 30.

The vjth of Januarie was bapt^d Elizabeth & Avis Daughters of Andrew Humfray.

The 31th of Januarie was bapt^d Ann Place Daughter of John Place, sen.

The same Daie was bapt^d Edward Brodstreet son of John Brodstreete.

D*

The i3th of ffeb was bapt^d Thomas Loue son of Edwarde Loue.
The xxth of March was bapt^d Martha Rucke Daughter of Cirriac Rucke.
Thus far certified the xijth of Aprill 1602.

Here entreth the yere of our L. 1602.

The xxvth of Aprill was baptiz. Marie Adye Daught^r of Mathye Adye.
The 2^d of May was baptiz. Marie Lyllye, Baseborne.
The same Daie was bapt^d Henrie Prise son of Mathew Prise.
The 9th of May bapt^d Grace Brockwell Daught^r of Richard Brockwell.
The 16th of May bapt^d Thomas Tayler son of Daniell Tayler.
The 23th of May bapt^d Stephan Norman son of Edw: Norman.
The same Day bapt^d Ann Smithson Daughter of John Smithson.
The 4th of Julye bapt^d Peter Juce son of Stephan Juce.
The first of August bapt^d Edward Shroubsoll son of Christopher Shroubsoll, Ju.
The 22th of August bapt^d Joan Nox Daughter of John Nox.
The 29th of August bapt^d Elizabeth Shroubsoll daughter of Thomas Shroubsoll, Ju.
The 3^d of October bapt^d Margerie Handley daught^r of Tho: Handley.
The ioth of Octob^r bapt^d Mathew Butler the son of Mathew Butler.
The 7th of Novemb^r bapt^d Ann Hills Daught^r of Michaell Hills.
The 2i^h of Noueber bapt^d Alice Spencer daught^r of Wiłłm Spencer.
The 6th of Decemb^r bapt^d William Collens son of Edward Collens.
The 24th of December bapt^d Thomas Juce son of Marke Juce baseborne.
The 26th of December bapt^d Thomas Tatersoll son of Christop: Tatersoll.
The 23th of Januarie bapt^d Elizabeth Place daughter of Wm Place.
The same day bapt^d Marie Porredge Daughter of Thomas Porredge.
The same Day bapt^d Edward Shroubsoll son of Edward Shroubsoll.
The 30th of Januarie bapt^d Edward Maxsted son of John Maxsted, Ju.
The same day baptized Abram Place son of John Place, sen.
The 2th of feb. was bapt^d Dorthye Golson daught^r of John Golson.

Page 31.

The 24th of feb bapt^d Ann Packnam daughter of Roger Packnam.
The 6th of March bapt^d Hamon Stenyng daughter of Christop Stenyng.
The 13th of March bapt^d Wm Howesse son of Richard Howesse.
The same Daie bapt^d Tomsyu Shoubsoll Daught^r of Edward Shroubsoll, sen.
The 20th of March bapt^d Ann Goose Daughter of Thomas Goose.

Here entreth the yere of our Lord 1603 1603 1603.

The 25th of March bapt^d ffrances Petyte Daughter of Henrie Petyte, gent.
The 10th of Aprill baptiz. John Greene, baseborne.
Thus far certified the 6th of May 1603.

The 29th of May baptiz. Ursula Best daughter of John Best gentn.
The 26th of June baptd Edward Travesse son of Edward Travesse.
The 16 of August baptd John Adie son of Mathie Adie.
The 4th of Septēbr baptd William Rye son of Christopher Rye.
The same Day baptd Elizabeth Brodstreet daughtr of John Brodstreete.
The 9th of Octobr baptd Joan Day Daughtr of John Day.
The 16th of Octobr baptd Tho : Norcote son of Tho : Norcote.
The 23th of Octobr baptd Thomas Shroubsoll son of Christopher Shroubsoll, sen.
The same Daie bapt. Tomsyu Shroubsoll Daught. of Christopher Shroubsoll.
The 28th of Octobr baptd Marie Kid, baseborne.
The 30th of Octobr baptd Thomas Wood son of Wm. Wood.
The same Daie baptd Elizabeth Kennard Daughtr of John Kennard.
The 6th of Nouēbr baptd Edward Preble son of Edward Preeble.
The 13th of Nouēber baptd Joan Pope Daughter of Thomas Pope, Ju.
The same Daie bapt. Joan Shroubsoll Daughter of (*sic*)
The 25th of Decēber baptd Marie Jacob Daughtr of Cir. Jacob.
The 18th of March baptd Edward Golson son of Edward Golson.

Here entreth the yere of our Lord 1604 1604.

The 25th of March bapt. Robt White son of . . . White.
The 8th of Aprill baptd William Loue son of Edward Loue.
The same Daie bapt. Thomsyn Collens daught. of Edw : Collens.
The 23th of May baptd Ann Loue daughter of George Loue.
The 27 of May baptd Tomasyn Norman daughtr of Edw : Norman.
The same Daie bapt. Thomas Mercer son of . . . Mercer.
The first of July bapt. Susan Downe Daughtr of Edw : Downe.
The same day bapt. Dennis Juce Daughtr of Stephan Juce.
The 8th of July baptd Margerie Wise Daughtr of Wm Wise.
The same Daie bapt. Thomas Penistone son of Tho : Penistone.
The 29 of July baptd Willm Cornish son of Laurence Cornish.
The 5th of August bapt. Marie Packnam Daughtr of Roger Pecknam.
The 12th of August bapt. Willm Hills son of Jeffry Hills.
The iijth of August bapt. Thomsyn Brockwell daughtr of Richard Brockwell.
The 16th of August bapt. Elizabeth Shroubsoll Daughter of Richard Shroubsoll.

WM. PLACE.

Page 32.

The first of Sept. bapt. John Prise son of Mathew Prise.
The 26th of Sept. bapt. Thomas Pantry son of Georg Pantry.
The same day baptd Robt son of a stranger.
The 11th of Nouēbr bapt. Edmund Hurst son of John Hurst.
The 18th of Nouēbr Anne Norcote Daught. of Thomas Norcote.
The 30th of Decemb baptd Edward Place son of Willm Place.
The 6th Januar. baptd Richard Shroubsoll son of Tho : Shroubsoll.
The same Daie bapt. Willm ffroud son of Joseph ffroud.

The 3ᵈ of feb baptᵈ Richard Daw son of John Daw.
The 24ᵗʰ of ffeb baptᵈ Water Mount son of Richard Mount.
The same Daie bapt. Marke Tayler son of Daniell Tayler.
The same Daie bapt. Margaret Rucke Daughtʳ of Cir. Ruck.
The 3ᵈ of March baptᵈ Margaret Lewes Daughtʳ of James Lewes.

                Thus far certified.

    Here entreth the yere of oʳ L. 1605 1605 1605.

The xxvᵗʰ of March was bapt. Alice Porredge Daughter of Thomas
    Porredge.
The 14ᵗʰ of Aprill baptᵈ Edw : Howesse son of Richard Howesse.
The 21ᵗʰ of Aprill baptᵈ Alice Thomas Daughtʳ of John Thomas.
The same Daie baptᵈ Achilles Banks son of James Banks.
The 28ᵗʰ of Aprill baptᵈ Ann Spencer Daughtʳ of Wiłłm Spencer.
The 5ᵗʰ of May baptᵈ Ann Shroubsoll Daughter of Edward Shroubsoll.
The 20ᵗʰ of May was baptiz. Wiłłm Maxsted son of John Maxsted.
The 26ᵗʰ of May was baptiz. Ann ffynch Daughtʳ of John ffynch, gent.
The 2ᵈ of June baptiz. Austen Tilson son of Edward Tilson.
The 9ᵗʰ of June baptiz. Elizabeth Place Daughtʳ of John Place thelder.
The 14ᵗʰ of Julye baptiz. Moses Shroubsoll son of Edw : Shroubsoll.
The 4ᵗʰ of August baptᵈ Ann Shroubsoll Daughter of . . . Shroubsoll.
The 8ᵗʰ of Septēbʳ bapt. Wiłłm Rucke son of John Ruck.
The 16ᵗʰ of Septēbʳ baptᵈ Josias Woodwall son of Mathew Woodwall.
The same Daie bapt. Margaret Shroubsoll Daughter of Wiłłm
    Shroubsoll.
The sixt of Octobʳ bapt. Thomasyn Hills Daughtʳ of Michael Hills.
The 20ᵗʰ of Nouēbʳ baptᵈ John Brodstreet son of John Brodstreet.
The 8ᵗʰ of Decēbʳ baptᵈ Christopher Page son of John Page.
The xvᵗʰ of Decēbʳ Anthonie Golson son of John Golson.
The 29ᵗʰ of Decēbʳ bapt Ann Hix Daughter of John Hix.
The 23ᵗʰ of Januarie bapt. Edward Robynson baseborne.
The 2ᵈ of ffeb bapt. Ann Mañering Daughtʳ of . . . Mannering.
The 16ᵗʰ of ffeb bapt. Grace Loue Daughtʳ of Edward Loue.
The 16ᵗʰ of March baptᵈ Margaret Adie Daughtʳ of Adie.
The 23 of March bapt. Michaell Norryce son of Michaell Norrice.

        Here entreth 1606 1606.

The first of May bapt. Wᵐ Collyns son of Edward Collins.
The 18ᵗʰ of May bapt. Tho : Pope son of Mathew Pope.
The first of June bapt. Stephen Spencer son of Wm. Spencer.
The 9 of June bapt. Elizabeth Mount Daughtʳ of Richard Mount.
The 22ᵗʰ of June bapt. Mathew Rucke son Cir. Rucke.

Page 33.
The 20ᵗʰ of July bapt. Tho : Maxsted son of John Maxsted, Ju.
The 7ᵗʰ of Septeb bapt. Elizabeth Baker Daughtʳ of Christ. Baker.
The 4ᵗʰ of Sept. baptᵈ Georg Tayler son of Daniell Tayler.
The 21ᵗʰ of Sept. baptᵈ John Tayler son of Gedeon Tayler.

The 12th of Octob^r bapt. Christop. Shroubsoll son of . . . Shroubsoll.
The 2^d of Noueb^r bapt. Alice Shroubsoll Daught^r of Tho : Shroubsoll.
The 9th of Noueb^r bapt. John Woodwall son of Mathew Woodwall.
The same Daie bapt. Miles Golson son of Edmund Golson.
The same Daie bapt. Elizab : Knot Daught^r of Stephan Knot.
The 30th of Noueb^r bapt. Marg. Howesse Daught^r of Rich. Howesse.
The 22 of Deceb^r Catharine Pantry Daugh of Georg Pantry.
The first of Jan. bapt. Clement Wise son of Willm Wise.
The 15th of ffeb bapt^d Grace Porredg Daught^r of Tho : Porredge.
The same Daie bapt. John Burden son of . . . Burden.
The 22th of ffeb bapt. Ann Norcote Daught^r of Tho : Norcote.
The first of March bapt. Alice Place Daught^r of John Place.
The 15th of March bapt. Willm. Preble son of Willm Preble.

1607. 1607. 1607. 1607.

The 29th of March bapt. John Knat son of Elizab. Knat, base born.
The 7th of Aprill bapt. Tho : Prise son of Math : Prise.
The 29th of Aprill bapt. Tho : Down son of Edward Downe.
The 26th of Aprill bapt. Ann Hills Daught. of Jeffry Hills.
The 10th of May bapt. Christopher Shroubsoll son of Edward Shroubsoll.
The 17 of May bapt. Mildred Norman Daughter of Edw. Norman.
The 31th of May bapt. Isaac Mannering son of . . . Mañering.
The 7th of June bapt. John Place son of John Place theld^r.
The same Day bapt. Alice Tõmas Daught^r of John Tõmas.
The 16th of Septeb^r bapt. Ann Shroubsoll Daughter of Thomas Shroubsoll.
The 27th of Septeb^r bapt. Edmund Tylson son of Edward Tylson.
The 4th of Octob^r bapt. Ciriac Ball son of John Ball.
The 11th of Octob^r bapt. Cathar. Hix Daught. of John Hix.
The same Day bapt. Ann Shroubsoll Daught. of . . . Shroubsoll.
The 20th of Deceber bapt. Moses Shroubsoll son Richard Shroubsoll.
The 15th of Januar. bapt. Margaret Clyfe, Baseborne.
The 30th of Jan. bapt. Raynold Shroubsoll son of Wm Shroubsoll.
The same Day bapt. John Shroubsoll son of the same William.
The same Day bapt. Margaret Rucke Daught^r of Gabriell Ruck.
The 21th of feb bapt. Henrie Day son of John Day.
The 6th of March bapt. Marie Mount Daught^r of Rich : Mount.
The 13th of March bapt. Sara Woodwall Daught^r of Mathew Woodwall.

Thus far certified.

Here entreth the yere of our L. Ch. 1608   1608   1608.
The 3^d of Aprill bapt. Joan Loue Daught^r of Edw. Loue.
The 10th of Aprill bapt. Joan . . . Daught^r of . . .
The 12th of August baptiz. florence Nox daughter of John Nox.
The 11th of Septeb^r bapt. Martha Spencer daughter of W^m. Spencer.
The same day bapt. Joan Shroubsoll Daughter of Edward Shroubsoll.
The 16th of Octob^r bapt. Elizabeth Pope Daughter of Nicholas Pope.

The 23th of Octobr bapt. William Tucker son of Tho : Tucker.
The 6th of Novēbr bapt. Ann Brodstreet Daughtr of John Brodstreet.
The 20th of Novēbr bapt. Water Wood son of William Wood.
The 4th of Decēbr bapt. Joyce Place Daughter of William Place.
The 11th of Decēbr bapt. Tho : Norcote son of Thomas Norcote.
The 18th of Decēbr bapt. Joan King daughter of Christopher King.

Page 34.

The same Day bapt. John Travesse son of Edward Travesse.
The first of Januar. bapt. Ann Elnar daughtr of Edward Elnar.
The 12th of feb bapt. Phebe Spencer Daughter of . . . Spencer.
The 13th of feb bapt. Catharine Roper Daughter of Henrie Roper.
The 26th of ffeb bapt. Dennis burd Daughter of John Burd.
The same Day bapt. Elizabeth burd Daughter of the same John Burd.
The 22th of March bapt. Alice Hix Daughter of John Hix.

Thus far certifyed.

Here entreth the yere of our L. 1609   1609   1609.

The 26th of March bapt. Ann Woodwall, basborne.
The 9th of Aprill bapt. Ann fisher daughter of . . . fysher.
The 23th of Aprill bapt. Richard Howesse son of Richard Howesse.
The 3^d of May bapt. Richard Hills son of Michaell Hills.
The 7th of May baptiz. Thomas Golson the son of Edmund Golson.
The 5th of June baptiz. Tomsyn Gates Daughter of . . . Gates.
The 23th of Julye baptiz. Thomas Porredge son of Thomas Porredge.
The 27th of August baptiz. William Mount son of Richard Mount.
The same Day baptiz. Thomsyn Wallard daughter of Henrie Wallard.
The 3^d of Septembr bapt. Cirrihack Pope son of Thomas Pope.
The 10th of Septēbr bapt : Marie the Daughter of A poore travayling Irishman.
The 8th of Octobr bapt John Paine son of Thomas Paine, Clerk.
The 10th of Decembr bapt. Susan Tayler Daughter of Daniell Tayler.
The 14th of Januarie bapt : Ann ffryth Daughr of Thomas ffryth.
The 28th of Jan. bapt. Ann Ping Daughter of William Ping.
The 4th of feb bapt. Joan Place Daughter of John Place theldr.
The 18th of ffeb baptiz. Joan Pantry Daughter of Georg Pantry.
The 25th of ffeb bapt. Ann Jrons Daughter of John Jrons.
The 6th of March bapt. William and Sara Bensted son & daughter of John Bensted.
The 18th of March Georg Ruck son of Gabriell Rucke.
The same Day bapt. Priscilla Giles Daughter of Henrie Giles.

Thus far certified.

Here entreth the yere of our Lord God 1610   1610.

Page 35.

The 25th Day of March bapt. Marke White son of . . . White.
The first of Aprill bapt. Thomas Hills the son of Jeffry Hills.
The 15th of Aprill bapt. Jonathan son of John Hare.
The same Day bapt. Alice Loue Daughter of Edward Loue.

The 29th of Aprill bapt. Margaret Besant Daughter of Georg Besant.
The same day bapt. Marian Tayler Daughter of Gedeon Tayler.
The 27 of May baptz. Elizabeth Tilson Daughter of Edward Tylson.
The 2d of June baptiz. An Spencer Daughr of . . . Spencer.
The 17th of June bapt. Joan Brodstreet Daughtr of Christopher
Brodstreet.
The first of July was bapt. William Chillenden son of John Chillenden.
The 22th of August Bapt. Cirriack Wyte Daughtr of William Wyte.
The 2d of Septembr bapt. Elizabeth Downe Daughter of Edward
Downe.
The 16th of ffeb bapt. Amye Hills Daughter of Michaell Hills.
The 24th of Septeb bapt. Marie Woodwall Daughter of Mathew
Woodwall.
The 7th of Octobr bapt. Robert Spencer son of Robert Spencer.
The same Day bapt. John Juce son of James Juce.
The first of Nouembr bapt. Elizabeth Banks Daughtr of Bankes.
The 4th of Nouembr bapt. William Bond son of Thomas Bond.
The 29th of Novemb bapt. Elizabeth Hix Daughter of John Hix.
The 6th of Januarie bapt. Ann Pope Daughtr of thomas Pope.
The 20th of ffeb bapt. Mathew Spencer son of William Spencer.
The 27th of ffeb bapt. Thomas Place son of William Place, Clerk.
The 17th of March bapt. Owen Shroubsoll son of Thomas Shroubsoll.
The same Day bapt. John Crushin son of Romanie Chrushin.

Thus far certified.

Here entreth the yere of our L. 1611.
The 21th of Aprill bapt. Alice Brodstreet Daughtr of John Brodstreet.
The 28th of Aprill bapt. Henrie Shroubsoll son of John Shroubsoll.

Page 36.
The 5th of May bapt. Thomas Tucker son of Thomas Tucker.
The 19th of May bapt. Thomas King son of Christopher King.
The 18th of June bapt. Thomas White son of William White.
The 23th of June bapt. Thomas Shroubsoll son of Thomas Shroubsoll.
The 7th of Julye bapt. Michaell Norcote son of Thomas Norcote.
The same Day. bapt. Gregorie Prise son of Mathew Prise.
The sixt of Octobr baptized John Spencer the son of Adam Spencer.
The 13 of Octobr bapt. Elizabeth Howesse daughter of Richard
Howesse.
The xxth of October bapt. Thomas Elnar son of Edward Elnar.
The 24th of Novembr bapt. Susan Paine daughter of Thomas Paine.
The xvth of Decembr bapt. Susan Shroubsoll Daughter of William
Shroubsoll.
The xxvjth of Januarie bapt. bapt. Marie Greene.
The same day bapt. Richard Bensted son of Richard Bensted.
The 21 of feb bapt. Abigall Golson daughter of Edward Golson.
The sixt of March bapt. John ffyttell.

Thus far certified.

Here entreth 1612 1612.

The 29th March bapt. Susan Tayler daughter of Gedeon Tayler.
The 12th of Aprill bapt. Austen King son of Christopher King.
The 26th of Aprill bapt. William Porredg son of Thomas Porredg.
The 26th of Julye baptiz. Thomas Chillenden son of John Chillenden.
The same Day bapt. Avis Webb Daughter of . . . Webb.
The 2d of August bapt. Edward Joanes sonne of Robert Joans.
The same Day bapt. Robert Layton son of . . . Layton.
The same Day bapt. John Dowglasse son of John Dowglasse.
The 9th of August bapt. William Norman son of Edward Norman.
The 27th of August bapt. Walter Loue son of Edward Loue.
The same Day bapt. Thomas Paine son of Thomas Paine.
The 25th of October bapt. Alice Bensted Daughter of John Bensted.

Page 37.
The same Day bapt. Elizabeth Ball daughter of John Ball.
The 8th of Novemb bapt. Joseph Shroubsoll son of . . . Shroubsoll.
The 13th of decemb bapt. ffrancis Woodwall daughter of Mathew Woodwall.
The 20th of decemb bapt. Thomas Shroubsoll son of William Shroubsoll.
The 9th of Januarie bapt. Georg Loue.
The 14th of ffeb bapt. Georg Pope son of Thomas Pope.
Thus far certified.

Here entreth 1613 1613.
The 28th of March bapt. Sara Spencer daughter of Adam Spencer.
The 4th of Aprill bapt. Joan Hills daughter of Michael Hills.
The i8th of Aprill bapt. Marie fyttell Daughtr of . . . ffyttell.
The 14th of May baptized John Spenser son of Richard Spenser of Boughton Coop:
The 2th of July bap. Alice the Daughter of Thomas ffryth.
The 4th of July bapt. Mary Daughter of the said Thomas ffryth.
The 25th of July bap. Susan daughter Xpfer Brodstreet.
The 8th of August bapt. William Clifford son of Richard Clifford.
The 22th of August bapt: Dennice Brodstret daughter of John Brodstreet.
The same day bap. Margaret Shrubsole daughter of Richard Shrubsole.
The 18th of Septemb bap. Margaret Spencer daughter of Robert Spencer.
The same Daye bap. Rebecca Lewies daughter of Isaack Lewies.
The 3th of October bap. Edward Downe son of Edward Downe.
The same daye bap : Austen Carr son of Augusten Carr.
The 21th of Nouember bap. Thomas Bond sonne of Thomas Bond.
The same Daie Elizabeth Tucker daughter of Thomas Tucker.
The 28th of November baptd Bennet Shrubsole daughter of Edward Shrubsole.

The same Daie bap. . . . of Wm White.
The 2th of January Willm Spenser son of William Spenser was baptized.
The 23th of January bapt. Mary Pearse daughter of James Pearse.
The 13th Daye of March bap. Jooyce Place daughter of Willm Place, Preacher of God's Word ther.
The 3th of Aprill bap. Dorothie Price daught^r of Mathew Price.

Here entreth 1614.
The 26th of Aprill bapt. Elizabeth Hickes daughter of John Hicks.

Page 38.
The 1th of May baptized Mary Shrubsole Daughter of Thomas Shrubsole.
The 8th of May baptized Abraham Bensted sonne of Richard Bensted, Junior.
The 29th of Maye bap. ffrances Norcot Daughter of Thomas Norcott.
The 12th of June bapt. Mary daughter of Laurance Juice.
The 19th of June was baptized Anne Pordage Daughter of Thomas Pordage.
The 26th of June bap. John son of John Irons.
The 7th of August baptiz. Sara Poope Daughter of Mathewe Poope.
Anne the daughter of William Whitall Baptized the 25th of September 1614 ut supa.
The 4th daie of December was bap. Ann Meare Daughter of Leonard Meare.
The 18th Day of December was bapt. Edward Shrubsole son of Wm Shrubsole, Carpenter.
The 22th of January baptized Thomas son of Edward Watsonne.
The 29th of the same bap. Eliz. daught^r of Wm White.
The 19th Daie of ffebruarie batized Margareth the daughter of Adam Spenser.
The 19th of March baptized Hamon the son of John ffittell of the wood sid.
Certified thus fare.

Here entreth 1615.
The 2th Daie of Apprill was baptized William son of Nicholas Shrubsole.
The same daie was baptized Elizabeth Daughter of William Dane.
The 16th of Aprill bap : John Baker son of John Baker.
The 23th of Apprill baptized Elizabeth the daughter of Henry Arctarie.
The 30th Day of Aprill baptized Amie the Daughter of Nicholas Pecknam.
The 21th Daye of May baptized Thomas Ball sonne of John Ball.
The same Daie bapt. Sara Daughter of John Gateman.
The 11th of June baptized William Hils the son of Hercules Hilles.

The 9th Day of July was baptized Edward the sonne of Thomas Webb.

The 15th Daye of the same wer baptized Adam & Wm Spenser the sonnes of Richard Spencer Cop.

The 6th of August baptized Anne & Marie the Daughters of Christopher Shubsole of Scockete Hill being twynes.

Page 39. ·

The 20th Day of August bap : John son of Gidion Tayler.

The xth Daie of September baptized Robert son of Andrew Newman.

The 26th Daie of the same baptized Willm son of Xpofer Kinge.

The 22th of October baptiz. Christoph Bradstreet son of of Christoph Bradestreet.

The same Day ba. Joane the Daughter of James Boykett.

The 5th of Novemb bapt. Sara Daughter of Rober. Maxted of the Woodside.

The same Daie bap. Ann Daughter of William Gammon.

The 12th of the same bap. Elizabet Daughter of Thomas Poope.

The 26th daie of the same baptized Marie Daughter of Michaell Porter.

The 28th daie of Januarie baptized Robert son of Mathew Scott.

The same Daie baptized Margaret daughter of Edward Shrubsole of South street.

The 24th Day of ffebruarie baptized Amie the Daghter of Richard Clifford.

The 17th Daie of March baptized William Boyse the son of Mathew Boyse.

The 24th daie of the same bapt. John Spencer son of Robert Spencer.

Thus fare Directly set downe.

Heare entreth the yeare of or Lord 1616: 1616:

The 21th Daie of Aprill baptized Susan Daught^r of W^m ffraunce of Sellinge.

The 10th daie of Maye baptized Mary the Daughter of John Netter.

The 12th of the same bapt. Dorothie the daughter of Christoph Shrubsole.

The 2th daie of June baptized Walter Webb son of John Webbe.

The 9th daie of the same baptized Edward the son of John Bradstreet.

The 14th daie of July baptized Susan daughter of Jeferie Mollenger.

The 4th daie of August bapt. Willm sonne of Thomas ffrith.

The 15th of September bap. Elizabeth the daughter of Isaack Lewis.

The 6th daie of Januarie was baptized Elizabeth daughter of Adam Spencer.

Page 40.

The 2th Daie of ffebruarie baptized Johane the Daughter of Leonard Meare.

The same Day was baptized Pricilla the Daughter of John Irons.

The 9th Daye of ffebruary baptized Mary the Daughter of Edward Watson.

The 16th of ffebruary was baptized Peter Place the son of William Place Vicarius pochialis Eccleciæ de Boughton subtus le Bleane.

The 16th of March bapt. Mathew Marshall son of Daniell Marshall.

Here entreth the yeare of Lord 1617.

The 30th day of March was baptized Edward sonne of Robt. Maxted, Junior.

The 4th day of May bapt. Mary the Daughter of Augusten Carr.

The same day bapt. Mary daughter of William Dane.

The 18th of May baptized Martha the daughter of Nicholas Shrubsole.

The 22th of June was baptized Anne the daughter of Hercules Hilles.

The 20th of July baptized William and Stephen Pime the sonnes of Stephen Pime.

The 27th of July baptized Mary the daughter of Mathew Boyse.

The 3th of August bapt. John the sonne of Phillipe Cox an outedweller.

The 24th of August bapt. Richard the sone of Lattentor.

The 7th Daye of Septemb was baptized Robert Shrubsole the soñe of Henry Shrubsole.

The 28th day of September was baptized Edward the sonne of Xpofer Bradestreete.

The 5th Daye of October was bapt. Christopher Moune the son of Michaell Moone.

The 26th daye of October was baptized Sara Price daughter of Mathew Price.

The 30th daye of November was baptized Elinor the daughter of John Whatman.

The 21th of December bapt. John the son of Wm Pickeforke borne of a traveling woman at John Kings.

The 28th of December bapt. Reignould the son of Mathew Abraham & Margaret his wife.

The same day was baptized John Pope the sonne of Thomas Poope.

The 11th day of January was baptized Marie the daughter of Wm Shrubsoule Carpenter.

The 18th of the same bap. Joyce the daughter of John Greeneham.

The 25th day of January bapt. Thomas the sonne of Thomas Hobbs.

Page 41.

The 22th day of March baptized John Webb the son of John Webb.

The same day was baptized Thomas the son of Thomas Shrubsole de Hickmans.

Heare entreth the yeare of our Lord 1618.

The 5th day of Aprill bapt. Elizabeth Shrubsole the daught^r of John Shrub : Junior.

The 26ᵗʰ day of Aprill bapt. Elizabeth the daughter of Daniell Marshall.

The 12ᵗʰ day of July bapt. Elizabeth ffrith Daughter of Thomas ffrith.

The 16ᵗʰ day of August baptized Otnell the sonne of Edward Shrubsole of sowth street.

The same day bap. Robert the sonne of Gedion Tayler.

The 20ᵗʰ of Sept. bap. Thomas son of John Hendma.

The 27ᵗʰ day of September baptized Elizabeth Mount the daughtʳ of John Mount.

The 4ᵗʰ day of October Elizabeth Kyne the daughter of William Kyne.

The 11ᵗʰ day of October baptized Grace Boykett the daughter of James Boykett.

The same day was bapt. Johane Boys the daughtʳ of Mathewe Boys.

The 18ᵗʰ day of October bapt. Johane the daughtʳ of Richard Shrubsole.

The 25ᵗʰ of October bap. John son of John Chillenden, senr.

The first of Novemb bap. Nicholas son of Jeffery Mollenger.

The 8ᵗʰ day of November baptized Mary the Daughter of William Vane.

The 22ᵗʰ day of November baptiz. Alice daug. of Mathew Scott.

The 29ᵗʰ day of Novembʳ bap. John son of Michell Porter.

The same day. bap. Katherine daug. of Richard Clifford.

The 10ᵗʰ day of January bap. Henry son of Adã Spenser.

The same day bap. Elizabeth Daugħ of Tho : Webb.

The 24ᵗʰ of January bap. Wᵐ son of Daniell Pemble.

The 27ᵗʰ of January bap. James Richard and John the sonnes of Isaack Lewis.

The 14ᵗʰ of ffebruary bap. Magaret daug. of Wᵐ Bing.

The 28ᵗʰ of ffebr. bap. Anne daughter of Henry Bayley.

The same day bap. Joane daug. of John Bayker.

The 7ᵗʰ of March bap. Mary daug. of Hercules Hilles.

1619.

The 29ᵗʰ day of March bapt. Sarar Ore the daughter of Thomas Ore.

The same day bap. Nicholas & Elizabethe children of Anne Woodwall, widowe, baseborne.

The 11ᵗʰ day of Aprill bapt. John Gatemã the sonne of John Gateman.

The 25ᵗʰ day of Aprill bapt. Susana the Daughter of John Downe.

The 29ᵗʰ of Aprill bapt. Susan the daug. of Symon Paramor.

The 9ᵗʰ of May bap. James Whatman the sonne of John Whatman.

The same day was bapt. Edward the sonne of John Mylles.

The 20ᵗʰ day of June bapt. John the sonne of Robert Maxted of Crooch.

Page 42.

The 4ᵗʰ of July baptized Margaret the daughter of John King.

The 18ᵗʰ day of July bapt. John the sonne Nicholas Hames.

The 15th day of August bapt. ffrances Hilles the daughter of William Hilles.

The 29th day of August bapt. Stephen Cox the sonne of Phillip Cox.

The 19th of September bapt. George Shrubsole son of Willm Shrubsole, Carpenter.

The same day was bapt. John Shrubsole son of Henry Shrubsole.

The 26th of Sept. bapt. Susan the Daughter of Valenten Ryder.

The 9th of Octob^r bapt. Elizabeth the daugh. of Joane Wild, baseborne.

The 10th day of Octob. bap. Henry Walard son of Thomas Walard.

The same day was bap. John Shrubsole son of John Shr, Junior.

The 24th of Oct. bapt. Wm Car son of Augusten Car.

The 21th day of Novemb baptized Judeth the daughter of Moses Pecknam.

The 2th day of December baptized Margaret the daughter of Avice Marshall, Baseborne.

The 12th of December baptized Katharine the daugh. of Richard Maxted Senex.

The 9th day of Januarie bapt. Margaret the daughter of John Webb.

The 16th of January bapt. Adam son Adā Spencer.

The same day bapt. Joane the daugh. of Wm Meares.

The 30th of January bap. Anne daugh. of Rich Lattenten.

The 20th day of ffebruary bapt. John Hobbs the sonne of Thomas Hobbes.

The 19th day of March baptized Anne Meare the daughter of Leonard Meare.

Here entreth the yeare of our Lord 1620   1620.

The 26th day of March baptized Elizabeth the Daughter of Nicholas Shrubsole.

The 2th day of Aprill bapt. John the sonne of Henry Gylles.

The same day bapt. Susan the daughter of John Adames of ffyshpyn.

The 9th day of Aprill was baptized John Evans the sonne of Thomas Evans.

The 16th day of Aprill was bapt. Elizabeth Chillenden the daughter of John Chillenden, senior.

The 30th day of Aprill was bapt. Robert Clifford the sonne of Richard Clifford.

The 2th of May was baptized John Binge the sonne of William Binge.

The 14th of May bapt. Wm Connaway the sonne of William Connaway.

The 24th of May bapt. Edward Maxted the son of Ezechiell Maxted.

The 6th of June bapt. Sara the daughter of John Brodstreete.

The 10th of June bapt. Elizabeth Shrubsole the Daughter of Edward Shrubsole of Boughton street.

The 11th of June bapt. Mary the daughter of Edward Bradford.

Page 43.

The 29th of June baptized Robert Baker ye sonne of Robert Baker.

The same day was baptiz. Marian the daughter of Richard Mount, an outdweller.

The 2^d of July was bapt. John Watson the sonne of Edward Watson.

The same day was bapt. Richard Pope the son of Thomas Poope.

The 9th day of July bapt. John Bensted the sonne of Richard Bensted, Junior.

The 27th day of August bapt. Priscilla Price the daughter of Mathew Price.

The same day bapt. Susana Savorie the daughter of Richard Savorie.

The same day bapt. Jane the daughter of Jefferie Mollenger.

The 17th of September baptized William Newneham the son of Andrew Newneham.

The first day of October baptized Jobane Pordage the daughter of Thomas Pordage.

The 8th day of October bapt. Mary Cooke the daught^r of Alexander Cook.

The 12th Day of Octob^r baptized Ann Shroubsole the Daughter of John Shrubsole, at nuttree.

The 29th Day of October was baptized Sara Carr the Daughter of Augusten Carr.

The 5th day of Novemb^r bapt. James Place the sonne of Henry Place, an outdweller.

The 26th day of Novemb^r bapt. Robert ffittell the sonne of John ffittell.

The 27th day of Novemb^r was baptized Edward Wood the sonne of Richard Wood.

The 24th Day of Decemb^r bapt. Ann Baseden the daughter of Sarā Baseden.

The 4th Day of January bapt. Mercy Baker the Daughter of John Baker.

The 5th day of January baptized Humfry Tufton the sonne of Sr Humfry Tufton, Knight.

The 18th daye of ffebruarie baptized John Prebble the sonne of Thomas Prebble.

The 26th day of ffebruary baptized Michaell Greenestreete the son of Richard Greenstreete, borne of a travalinge woman.

The 4th of March was baptized Anne Downe the daughter of John Downe.

The same Day was baptized Mary Shrubsole the Daughter of Thomas Shrubsole.

The 11th day of March was baptized Dorothie the daughter of John Gateman, an outdweller.

The 18th of March was bapt. Joane Keane the daught^r of William Keane.

Heare entreth the yeare of our Lord Christ 1621.
The 25ᵗʰ of March was bapt. Priscilla Bayley the daughtʳ of Henry Bayley.
The 2ᵗʰ day of Aprill was baptized Mary Ockenfold the daughter of Edward Ockenfold.
The 15ᵗʰ of Aprill ·was baptized Elizabeth Marche the daughter of John March, Junior.
The same Day was baptiz Joane Hilles the daughter of Hercules Hilles.
The 22ᵗʰ of Aprill was bapt. George the sonne of . . . Wallerd.
The same day was bapt. Mildred Shrub: the daughtʳ of Joyce Shrubsole, widowe, base borne.
The 3ᵗʰ day of June was baptized John Dane the sonne of William Dane.

Page 44.
The first day of July was baptized Elizabeth Whatman the daughter of John Whatman.
The 17ᵗʰ day of July was baptized John Hẽman the sonne of John Hẽman.
The same day was baptized ffrances Binge the daughter of William Binge.
The 9ᵗʰ day of September was bapt. John Meares the sonne of Williã Meares.
The 16ᵗʰ of September was baptized Thomas Scott the sonne of Mathew Scott.
The 13ᵗʰ daie of October was baptized Williã Spenser the sonne of Robert Spenser.
The 18ᵗʰ day of October was baptized Avis Maxted the daughter of Ezechiell Maxted.
The 28ᵗʰ day of Octoбʳ bapt. Mary Marshall the daughter of Daniell Marshall.
The 4ᵗʰ day of Nouembʳ baptiz. Archelaus Hilles the sone of William Hilles.
The 9ᵗʰ of Nouembʳ bapt. Elizabeth Porteʳ Daughter of Michaell Porter.
The 18ᵗʰ of Novembʳ bapt. Susana the daughter of Mathew Boys.
The 16ᵗʰ of Decembʳ baptized Elenor Shrub: the daughter of Henrie Shrubsole.
The 27ᵗʰ day of Januarie was baptized Dorithie Brockwell the daughter of James Brockwell.
The 24ᵗʰ of ffebruary bapt. Edward the sonne of Edward Shrubsole, of Sowth streete.
The same day was bapt. Thomas Johnson the sonne of Jehu Johnson.
The same Day was bapt. Sara the daugh. of Valenten Ryder.
The 11ᵗʰ day of March was bap: Alice Wood the daughter of Ricbard Wood.
The 20ᵗʰ day of March was bapt. Anne Greenehã the daughter of John Greeneham.
E

Heere entreth the yeare of our Lord 1622.

The 25th day of March Anno Dom 1622.

The 22th of Aprill bap : Eliz : the Daughter of Job Bircher.

The 28th day of Aprill was baptized Edward Scott the sonne of Thomas Scott.

The same Day was baptized Edward Clifford the sonne of Richard Clifford.

The 5th of May bap. ffrauncis the sonne of Robert Baker.

The 2th day of June baptized Elizabeth Place the Daughter of Henry Place, outdweller.

The 7th Day of July was baptized Dennice Webb the Daughter of John Webb.

The 25th day of August bap^{d} Elizabeth Shrubsole the daughter of Edward Shrubsole of Boughton streete.

The first day of September bap. William Shrubsole son of Williã Shr : of northlane.

The 8th of Septemb^{r} was bapt. John Kinge son of John Kinge.

The 10th of Septemb^{r} bapt. Anne Spenc Daughter of Robert Spencer.

The 29th day of Sept bapt. Priscilla Merch the daughter of John m̃ch the yonger.

The 6th of Octob^{r} bapt. Elizabeth Hẽman the daughter of John Henman, posthumus.

The same day was bapt. Susan Brooke the daught of John Brooke.

The 13th day of Octob^{r} bapt. John Barr sonne of John Barr.

The first day of January bap : George Sherlock sonne of John Sherlocke, Junr.

The 6th of January bapt^{d} Susana Spencer daughter of Adam Spencer.

Page 45.

The 12th day January baptized Joane Mount the daught^{r} of John Mount.

The 23th day of January bapt. Wm Binge sonne of William Bynge.

The 2th Day of ffebruary was baptized Edward the sonne of Henry Shrubsole.

The 9th day of ffebruary baptized George the sonne of John Shrubsole of Sowth street.

The same day was James sonne of Isaacke Lewies.

The 16th day of ffebruary was baptized Anne Mount the daughter of Richard Mount, an outdweller.

The 9th day of March bapt. Robert Tritton sonne of Robert Tritton.

The 23th day of March was baptized ffrances Hilles Daughter of Hercules Hilles.

1623.

The 30th of March baptized Richard Baker the sonne of John Baker.

The 6th of Aprill baptized Anne Wallard daughter of Thomas Wallard.

The 4th day of Aprill was baptized John Tufton the sonne of Sr Humfry Tufton, Knight.

The 22th day of May was baptized Leonarde Mears the Sonne of Leonard Mears.

The 10th day of August was baptized Elizabeth Pordage daughter of Thomas Pordage.

The 5th of Octob baptized . . . Evance . . . Evance.

The 19th of Octob baptized John Okenfold son of Edward Okenfold.

The 16th of Noueb. baptized Raynold Maxsted son of Ezechiell Maxsted.

The 7th of Decemb^r baptized Elizabeth Wood daughter of Richard Wood.

The 21th of Decemb^r baptized Margaret Baker daughter of Nicholas Baker.

The 6th of Januarie baptized Susan Spencer daughter of Adam Spencer.

[*Half the page cut away but apparently before any entries had been made.*]

Page 46.

The 18th of Januarie bapt. Thomas Penn sonne of Wm Penn.

baptized the same daie John Brenchlie son of Richard Brenchlie.

The 16th of feb baptized James Marshall son of Daniell Marshall.

The same daie bapt. Richard ffittell son of Richard ffittell.

The 23th of ffeb baptized Elizabeth Cooke daught^r of Roger Cook.

The Last daie of feb bapt. Tho: Binge son of Tho: Bing.

The 14th of March bapt. Daniel Rid^r son of Valentine Rider.

1624.   1624.

The 25th of March bapt. Wm Cook son of Thomas Cook.

The year of our Lord 1624.   1624.

The 4th of aperel was baptised Wiliam shrubsol sonne of Edward Shrubsol.

the same day was baptised Joane Prebell daughter of thomas Prebell.

baptised the eleuen day of aperel Sarah forset daughter of John forset.

the seuenteenth day of aperell was baptised william Clifford sonn of Richard Cliford.

the therteenth day of Aperell was baptised Joane brooke dauther of John brooke.

the eighteenth day of apel was baptised Renight maxsted sonn of samewell maxsted.

The 25 of Apel was baptised Edward fperiman sonn of thomas fperiman.

the same daie was baptised allis gatman dauthter.

The 30 day of may was baptised thomas Goos sonn of thomas Goos.

The 10 day of Jun was baptised mary the Daughter of Edward Shrubsoll.

The 20 Day of Jun was baptised margaret mount Daughter of Richard mount.

[*Half the page cut away, but no evidence of entries lost.*]

E²

MARRIAGES.

Page 47.   Here beginneth the yere of our Lord 1558.
The 14ᵗʰ day of June was marryed Nicholas Lull to Joan Easton.
The 21ᵗʰ of June were married Rychard Shroubsoll & Avis Claye.
The 7ᵗⁱ of Julye were married Christopher Hud & Alice Jefferye.
The 17ᵗʰ of Julye were married Christopher Chapman & Oliue Bendland.
The xvjᵗʰ of Januarie were married Edward Songer & Ann Ragnold.

Here entreth the yere of our Lord 1559.
The 22ᵗʰ of May were married Wiłłm Bayley & Ann . . .
The 23ᵗʰ of May were married John Best & Marie Porredge.
The 19ᵗʰ of June were married Rychard ffarnam & Ann Sutton.
The same Daie were married John Best & Ann Harris.
The xᵗʰ of Septēbʳ was married Davye Joanes.
The 18ᵗʰ of Septēbʳ was married Rich : Norman (*sic*).
The iiij of Decēbʳ was married Richard Norman (*sic*).
The ixᵗʰ of Decēbʳ were married Rychard Tomison & Ann ffennett.

Here entrethe the yere of our Lord 1560.
The 20ᵗʰ of May was married John Waller.
The first of ffebruarie were married Markes Pecknam & Julyan Aberrye.

Here entreth the yere of our Lord 1561.
The 8ᵗʰ of June were marryed John Maxsted & Elizabeth Grimsell.
The ixᵗʰ of June were maryed Edward Hammon & Joan Rucke.
The 7ᵗʰ of Julye were married John Stephins & Elizabethe . . . .
     (*name obscured by a blot of ink*).
The xxvᵗⁱ of Septēbʳ were marryed Wiłłm Smyth of Hodsden in
     Hartfordshire & Alice field.
The last of Septēbʳ were married John Spencer & Alyce Norman.
The 17ᵗʰ of Nouēmbʳ were married Edward Allen & Jssabell Littlewood.
The first of Decēbʳ were married Mathie Jacob & Avis Tennaker.
The 23ᵗʰ of Januarie were married Thomas Burnell & Seth Bygg.

Here entreth the yere of our Lord 1562.
The xxᵗʰ of Julye were married John May & Alice Pantrye.
The 27ᵗʰ of Julye were married Christopher Denslake & Alice Rider.
The vᵗʰ of October were married Stephan Porredge & Elizabeth
     Blankett.
The xiijᵗʰ of October were married Rychard Shroubsoll & Elizabeth
     Maxsted.
The 21ᵗʰ of Octoƀʳ were married Wiłłm Laurence & Joan Wylcockes.
                                        WILLIAM PLACE.
                                        RICHARD RUCKE.
                                        THOMAS HENDMAN. ⊕

Page 48. Here entreth the yere of our Lord 1563.

The ₂₂ᵗʰ of June were married Nicholas Hayward & Elizabeth Ⓟₕ₂ₐᵢₗᵖp.

The xᵗʰ of June were married John Preston & Joan Luke.

The 7ᵗʰ of Octobʳ were married John Cowp & Ann Blankett.

The 27ᵗʰ of Octob were married John Woodwall & Ann Catell.

The xxviᵗʰ of Januarie were married Edward Hammond & Joan Haukyns.

Here entreth the yere of our Lord 1564.

The xiijᵗʰ of Nouẽbʳ were married Laurence Man & Ann Barbar.

The xijᵗʰ of ffeb were married Thomas Pope & Elizabeth Burge.

Here entrethe the yere of our Lorde 1565.

The 26ᵗʰ Daie of May were married John Legatt & Margerye Sympson.

The xxvᵗʰ of June were married John Head & Ann Momforthe.

The xxiᵗʰ of Julye were married Edward Brodstreete & Elizabeth Dod.

The 8ᵗʰ of October were married Henrie Powell & Ellionor Scott.

The 22ᵗʰ of Octobʳ were married Roger Alyn & Alice Knot.

The 26ᵗʰ of Nouẽbʳ were married Rychard Shroubsoll & Chrystian Browne.

Here entreth the yere of our Lord 1566.

The iiij of Julye were married Simon Dylett & Ann Cacherell.

The 27ᵗʰ of Julye were married John Tennaker & Alyce Juce, widow.

The iiijᵗʰ of Nouember were married John Haukes & Ann Mare.

The 24ᵗʰ of Nouember were married Wiłłm Maxsted & Joan Okenfold.

The 22ᵗʰ of Januarie were maried Rychard Lewis & Margaret Haukyns.

Here entreth the yere of our Lord 1567.

The xxvᵗʰ of August were married Henrie Whetstone & Marye Best.

The 18ᵗʰ of Septẽbʳ were married John Balden & Ann Barr.

The 24ᵗʰ of ffebruarie were married Thomas Brewer & Joan Hamon.

Here entrethe the yere of our Lord 1568.

The 22ᵗʰ of Julye was married John Cowper.

Here entreth the yere of our Lord 1569.

The xiᵗʰ of June was married Thomas Chamerlane.

The 6ᵗʰ of Octobʳ were married Wyllyam Blankett & Ann Shroubsoll.

Here entreth the yere of our Lord 1570.

The 28ᵗʰ of June were marᵈ John ford & Bennet Parker.

The 30ᵗʰ of Octobʳ were marᵈ Mathew Lyat & Margᵗ Bayley.

The 13ᵗʰ of Nouēbʳ were marᵈ Henrie Raynold & Joan Place.
The 23 of Nouēbʳ were marᵈ John Bradford & Christian Jerman.
The —ᵗʰ of Nouēbʳ were married John Rucke & Susan Haukyns.
The 18ᵗʰ of December were married Nicholas ffynch & Dorothie
Ingham.

> WILLIAM PLACE.
> RICHARD RUCKE.
> THO : HENDMAN. ⊕

Page 49.

Here endeth the old Register : from the xxviiiᵗʰ of December 1570 to
the ixᵗʰ of June 1572 ther is noe Marriages to be found in our
church bookes.

Here entreth the yere of our Lord, 1572.

The ixᵗʰ of June were married Peter Koke & ffryset Keeler.
The 19ᵗʰ of June were married James Car & Margaret Wylmontnige.
The 27ᵗʰ of Julye were married John Tucker & Joan Louker.

Hitherto the names ar exhibited to yᵉ Ordinarie.

Here entreth the yere of our Lord 1573.

The 14ᵗʰ of Julye were married Nicholas Upton & Parnell Amys.
The xxᵗʰ of Julye were married Thomas Maxsted & Dennis
Shroubsoll, widow.
The 6ᵗʰ of ffeb were married Andrew More & Ann Byrd, wid.

Thus far exhibited to yᵉ ordinarie.

Here entreth the yere of our Lord, 1574.

The 22ᵗʰ of Julye were married Wiłłm Chillenden & Zacharie
Howesse.
The 30ᵗʰ of Julye were married John Hussye & Catharine Adie.
The xijᵗʰ of Septēbʳ were married Thomas Haukyn the youngʳ and
Ann Pettyt.
The xviijᵗʰ of Octobʳ were married Stephan Bensted & Alyce Browne.
The 14ᵗʰ of ffeb were married Bensted & Ann Bontyng.
The same Day were married Andrew Owen & Alyce Crambroke.

Here entreth the yere of our Lord, 1575.

The 21ᵗʰ of Aprill were married John Cornish & Ann Denslake wid.
The 14ᵗʰ of Octobʳ were married Christopher Raynolds & Margaret
Place.
The 30ᵗʰ of Januar. were married John Raynolds & Christian . . .
The xxixᵗʰ of Octobʳ were married Wiłłm Preston & Catharine
Raynolds.

Here entreth the yere of our Lord 1576.

The 26ᵗʰ of Nouēbʳ were married Willyam Dale & Christian
Shroubsoll.

Here entreth the yere of our L. 1577.

The first of May were married Rychard Perkyn & Florence Dunkyn.

The 2ᵈ of June were married Rychard Maxsted & Susan Hills.

The 22ᵗʰ of Julye were married Stephan Bensted & Julyan Perknam.

The 2iᵗʰ of Octobʳ were married John Shroubsell & Margerie Juce.

WILLIAM PLACE.
RICHARD RUCKE.
THO : HENDMAN. ⊕

Page 50.

The 30ᵗʰ of December were married John Dryland and Elizabeth Pettyt.

The 20ᵗʰ of Januarie were married Raynold Alrund and Tomsyn Norman.

Here entreth the yere of our L. 1578.

The 30ᵗʰ of June were married John Plott and Julyan Shroubsell.

The 20ᵗʰ Julie were married Jeames Bucke and Christian Wihall.

The 24ᵗʰ of Septẽbʳ were married John Burton & Joan Parker.

The 3ᵈ of Nouẽbʳ were married James Carr and Marie Murton.

The 30ᵗʰ of Nouẽbʳ was married Davye Harris & Elizabeth Peny-stone.

Here entreth the yere of our L. 1579.

The 18ᵗʰ of May were married Thomas Kempe, & Joan Clyfford.

The 19th of Octobʳ were married Rychard Maxsted & Ellen Davye.

The 29ᵗʰ of October were married Adam Rucke & Alice fforward.

Here entreth the yere of our L. 1580.

The 25ᵗʰ of May were married John Legat and Elizabeth Berrye.

The 24ᵗʰ of Octobʳ were married Thomas Throwley and Elizabeth Colwell.

The 26ᵗʰ of Nouẽbʳ were married William Allen and Alice Throwleye.

The 19ᵗʰ of Januarie were married Thomas Keeler & Alice Jnge.

The 23ᵗʰ of Januarie were married Richard Handley & Ellenor Shroubsoll.

Here entreth yᵉ yere of our L. 1581.

The 3ᵈ of Aprill were married John ffryar and Elizabeth Bayston.

The 20ᵗʰ of Aprill were married Philipp Cornish and Alle Chapman.

The 20ᵗʰ of Julie were married Willm Shroubsoll & Tomsyn Ellis.

The 29ᵗʰ of Octobʳ were married Laurence Brooke & Ann Tedman.

The 5ᵗʰ of Nouẽbʳ were married Hamon Watson and Florence Songer.

The 27ᵗʰ of Nouẽbʳ were married Mathew Heler & Barbarow Howesse.

The same Daie were married William Clyfford & Joan Corbet.

The same Daie were married Thomas Woollan and Mildred Bryce.

The 29ᵗʰ of Januarie were married Nicholas Juce & Alice Clyfford.

The 20ᵗʰ of ffeb were married Mathie Clifford & Jane fynche.

Here entreth the yere of our L. 1582.
The 11th of June were married Arthure ffringe & Martha Rucke.

WILLIAM PLACE.
RICHARD RUCKE.
THOMAS HENDMAN. ⊕

Page 51.

The 8th of Noueb^r were married John Balden and Parnell Clyfford.
The same Daie were married Nicholas Hannington & Tõsyn ffarnam.
The 28th of Nouēbr were married Stephan Swan and Elizabeth Balden.
The 21th of Januarie were married Wiłłm Okenfold & Margaret Juce.
The 24th of Januarie were married Mathew Marshall & Susan Beale.

Here entreth the yere of our L. 1583.
The 4th of Julie were married Edward Dunkyn and Phebe Dickinson.
The 29th of Julie were married Peter Rucke and Anne Matryce.
The 3^d of Octob^r were married William Browne and Joan Hanniñg.
The 12th of Octob^r were married Thomas Littlewood & Joan Tryce.
The 10th of feb were married John Adamer and Joan Tennaker.
The 13th of feb were married Robt Clyfford and Ann Abberrye.
The 15th of feb were married William Palmer and Elizabeth Throwleye.
The 2d of March were married John Golson and Ann Dine.

Here entreth the yere of our L. 1584.
The 20th of Julie were maried Thomas Browne and Alice Pryne.
The 26th of Nouēb^r were married John Collen and Christian Raynolds.
The 3^d of feb were married Cirriacke Rucke and Margaret Carter.

Here entreth ye yere of our L. 1585.
The 13th of June were married James Lewes and Ann Gray.
The 29th of Octob^r were married Thomas . . . and Margerie Roger.
The 17th of Januarie were married Robt. Swyft and Margaret Pemble.
The 24th of Januarie were married James Scott & Joan Jacob.

Here entreth the yere of our L. 1586.
The 30th of Maie were married Laurence Brooke and Alice Attur, wid.
The same Daie were married Thomas Goose and Joan Cornish.
The 13th of June were married Henrie Tomson and Joan Buddle.
The 20th of June were married John Edwards and Joan Roger.
The 26th of Julie were married Rychard Willoway & Marie Wingfield.
The 23th of Octob^r were married James Whatman and Ann Juce the Daught^r of William Juce.

WILLIAM PLACE.
RICHARD RUCKE.
THOMAS HENDMAN. ⊕

Page 52.

Here entreth the yere of our L. 1587.

The 20th of Nouēb^r were married Edward Hammon and Susan Jacob. The same Daie were married John Berrye and Ann Tennaker. The 28th of Nouēb^r were married John Smyth and Alice ffaireman. The 4th of Decēmb^r were married Austen Kyng and Margerie Segges.

Thus far certified.

Here entreth the yere of our L. 1588.

The 16th of feb were married Thomas Hunt and Jane Jetter. The 14th of Nouēb^r were married John Dane and Margerie Spencer. The 10th of Octob^r were married Thomas Purviour and Susan Wood. The same Daie were married William Shillyng and Mildred Essex. The 15th of Julye were married Edward Juce and Susan Shroubsoll.

Here entreth the yere of our L. 1589.

The 13th of Aprill were married Ralf Pantrye and Ann Collens. The 16th of Aprill were married John Blanket and Elizabeth Cornish, Wid. The 27th of Maie were married Robert Sharpe and Ann Osbyson. The 29th of May were married Georg Jeffrye and Alice Snod. The second of June were married John Place and Ellise Juce. The 30th of June were married Edward Tennaker and Ann Kyng.

Thus far certified.

The 16th of Octob^r were married Thomas Elsten and Marie Walles.

Here entreth the yere of our L. 1590.

The 28th of Septēb. were married John Kyng, Jun., & Catharine Presson, wid. The 4th of Octob^r were married James Bankes & Marie Knott. The 28th of Octob^r were married Thomas Norman and Ann Rucke, wid. The 16th of Nouēb^r were married John Knocke & Mildred Lyffet, wid. The first of December were married Rychard Rucke & Marie Porredg, wid.

Here entreth the yere of our L. 1591.

The 2d of Septeb^r were married Robt Gray and Ellenor Whitesyde.

Thus far certified the 28th of decemb^r.

Here entreth ye yere of our L. 1592.

The 24th of Nouēb^r were married Robert Maxsted and Rose Shroubsoll.

WILLIAM PLACE.
RICHARD RUCKE.
THOMAS HENDMAN. ⊕

Page 53.

The 27th of Nouẽbʳ were married Thomas ffaireman, and Joan Best, wid.

The 25th of Januarie were married William ffilcot and Joan Benkyn.

The 29th of Januarie were married Rychard Howesse and Ann Norman.

1593.   1593.   1593.

The xiiijth of May were married William Place, Cler., and Priscilla Jacob.

The 9th of Julie were married Wiłłm Shroubsoll, and Joan Clyfford.

The i3th of August were married Edward Dine, and Joan Kyng.

The 24th of Septẽbʳ were married Cirriack Jacob and Ann Berry, wid.

Thus far certified the 11th of Octobʳ 1593.

The 5th of Nouẽbʳ were married Roger Pecknam, and Tomsyn Sankyn.

The 26th of Nouẽbʳ were married John Kennard, and Marie Anncell.

The 28th of Januarie were married John Pye, and Ann Jacob.

Here entreth ye yere of our L. 1594.

The 8th of Aprill were married Thomas Horseley and Alice Brooke, wid.

The 13th of May were married Edward Shroubsoll & Ellenor Wylls.

The 23th of Septẽbʳ were married Jsraell Jerman and Margaret Spencer.

Thus far certified the ixth of Octobʳ 1594.

The 14th of October were married Michaell Hills and Ann Byx.

The 2ith of Octobʳ were married John Maxsted and Alice Shroubsoll.

The i2th of Januarie were married Henrie Joans & Joan Scott, Wid.

The last of Januarie were married Thomas Spencer, and Catharine ffinnis.

The same Daie were married Paule Spencer and Margerie Allen.

Here entrethe the yere of our L. 1595.

The 28th of Aprill were married John Nox & Marie Collyer.

The 22th of Maie were married John Ledger and Elizabeth Lowe.

The i6th of June were married John Maxsted and Elizabeth Lansfield.

The 24th of June were married Roḃt Sheep and Alice Anncell.

The 7th of Julie were married Thomas Hendman, and Jssabell Rucke, wid.

The 14th of October were married Wiłłm Cornish and Joan Longley, wid.

The 26th of Januarie were married Laurence Brooke, and Joan Hills, wid.

WILLIAM PLACE.
RICHARD RUCKE.
THOMAS HENDMAN. ⊕

Page 54.

The 24th of feb were married Thomas Porredge and Dorothie Drayton.

Here entreth the yere of o^r L. 1596.

The 2ith of June were married John Sweetyng, and Susan Bassett.
The 22th of Julie were married Rychard Trice and Margaret Dunkyn.

Thus far certified the 7th of Octob^r 1596.

The 29th of October were married Rychard Badkyn and Joan Golson.
The i8th of October were married Robt Obbyne, and Cicilla Dad, wid.

Here entreth the yere of o^r L. 1597.

The ioth of Julye were married Willm Ower, and Marie Rase.
The first of August were married Tho : Shroubsoll and Marie Pollard.

Thus far certified ye 11th of Octob^r 1597.

The 6th of Noueber were married Mathew Pope and Jssabell Presson.
The 2ith of Noueb^r were married Thomas Shroubsoll and Tomsyn Miller.
The 28th of feb were married Laurence Cornish and Joan Wood.

Here entrethe ye yere of o^r L. 1598.

The 17th of Julie were married Wm Shadwater and Margaret Bush.
The 7th of August were married Rychard Essex and Zacharie Chillenden.
The 29th of Octob^r were married John Golson & Rebecca Buckmer.
The 2ith of Septeb were married Willm Enfield and Ann Rucher.
The 6th of Noueb^r was maried Ralf Lane and Thomsyn Gregorie.
The i6th of Januarie was married Thomas Potter & Sara scoles.
The same Daie were married Thomas Prebble and Ellen Pemble.

1599.

The 24th of June were married Edward Goodgrome & Myldred Claygate.
The 29th of Julie were married Edward Collens & Sixborow Stiffe.
The 30th of Julye were married Edward ffȳn and Dorothie Shroubsoll.
The 5th of Nouember were married John Hethe & Jane Croyden, wid.
The same Day were married John Tong & Elizabeth Quilter.
The same Day were married Edward Downe & Ann Rucke.
The 19th of Nouemb were married Robt Maxsted & Ann Needes.

W_M. PLACE.

Page 55. ·

Here entreth the yere i6oo.

The 30th of June were married Christopher Stennings and Marie Downe.
The 7th of Julye were marryed John Everith and Margaret Chillenden.

The sixt of Octob^r were maried Allen Ellwen & Elizabeth Phesant.
The xxth of October were marryed Vyncent Howard & Susan Walden.
The 23th of Nouēb^r were married Edward Collens & Thomsyn Marten.
The xxvth of ffeb was married John Knocke & Susan Brodstreet.

Certified at Easter 160i.

Here entreth the yere of our Lord 160i.
The 22th of June were married John Shroubsoll and Joan Pemble.
The 9th of Julye were married Rychard Brockwell & Joan Badkyn, wid.
The 16th of Nouember were married Christopher Shroubsoll & Elizabeth Maxsted.
The 12th of Januarie were married John Edwards & Alice Cornish, wid.
The 15th of ffeb were married Rychard Bennett & Margarett Hills.
.thus far certified the 12th of Aprill 1602.

Here entreth the yere of our L. 1602.
The 12$^{·h}$ of Aprill weve married Edward Pope and Tomsyn Harker.
The last of May were maryed Henrie Athorn and Dorothye Mount.
The xiiij of June were maryed Georg Pantry and Alice Dine.
The i6 of Nouēber were maried Christopher Donnes & Joan Dine.

Thus far certified the 5th of May 1603. Yere of O^r Lord. 160;.

The first of August were married Richard Shroubsoll & Joyce Edwards.
The 28th of August were married Gylbert Stoughtō and Susan Basset.
The 2^d of Octob^r were married John Hix & Christian Lewes.
The 3^d of Octob^r married Andrew Dilock & Margaret Rucke.
The i3th of Octob^r married Thomas Penistone and Joan Scott.
The 23th of Januarie John Lawe and Ann Clement.

Here entreth the yere of our L. 1604.   1604.
The i6th of Aprill were married Richard Elsworth & Jane Gedger.
The 4th of June married Wittm Ashton & Phebe Dunkyn.
The 11th of June married Edward Tilson & Marie Hills.
The 9th of July married Abraham Bensted & Bennet Atkins.
The 25th of Octob maried Robt . . . & Marie Easton.
The 5th of Nouēb^r maried Edward Clifford & Avis Lewes.
The 19th of Nouēber maried John Balden & Catharine Hider.

Here entreth the yere of O^r L. god 1605.   1605.
Page 56.
The 15th of Octob married Thomas Hewes & Marie Peene.
The 17th of Octob married Abell Smyth & Avis Raynolds.
The 21th of Octob married Thomas ffowler & Elizabeth Adie, wid.

The 24 of Octob married Gedeon Tayler & Margaret Dandye.
The same Daie married John Grenham & Joan Mount.
The 5th of Nouebr married Richard Warren & Alice Basset.
The 18th of Nouebr married Georg Besant & Joan Sheffeild.
The 25th of Nouebr married Wm Shroubsoll & Susan Maxsted.
The 10th of ffeb married Edward Shroubsoll & Marie Hendman.

1606. 1606. 1606.

The 12th of May marryed Henrie Pemble & Tomsin Spencer.
The 12th of May marryed Sollomon Wilson & bethulia Baker.
The 12th of Julye marryed Thomas Pantry & Ann Bayley.
The 25th of July marr. Henrie Dilett & Marie Harris.
The 20th of Octob mar. John Silkwood & Joyce Claye.
The 17th of Nouebr mar. Willm ffrances & Susan Shrobsoll.
The 19 of Jan. married John Kennard & Ann Downe.
The 26th of Jan. married Adam Spencer & Elizab. Whatman.
The same Daie mar. Edmund Goffe & Joan Brooke.

1607. 1607. 1607.

The 28th of Aprill married John Jron & Cicilla Hussey.
The 18th of May mar. Beniamin Wood & Joan Raynolds.
The 3d of Octob Edward Elnar & Joan Tylson.
The 2d of ffeb mar. Christopher King & Elizabeth Brodstreet.

thus far certified.

1608. 1608.

The 4th of Aprill mar. Danyell Baker & Joan Woodwall.
The 30th of Octob mar. John Rayner & Sara Woodwall.

Thus far certified.

Here entreth 1609 1609.

The 20th of May marryed Christopher Downes & Thomsyn Latt, wid.
The 24th of July married Thomas Shroubsell & Catharine Wingfield.
The 24th of Septemb marr. Cyriack ffurnace & Joan Clarke.
The same Day marr. Edward Wise & Sara Hewes.
The 19th of Octob married John Chillenden & Joan Shroubsoll.
The 16th of Januarie marryed Isaack Lewes & Thomasyn Brooke.
The 22th of Januarie marryed John Whitehed & Dorothy Stevens.

Thus far certifyed.

Here entreth the yere 1610 1610 1610.

The 16th of Aprill marryed William Tith & Margaret Lashenden.
The 18th of June marryed John Juce & Dennis Juce, wid.
The 27 of Nouemb marryed Abram Cullen & Sara Bredge.
The 4th of ffeb maryed Thomas Lewes & Marie Spilman.

Thus far certifyed.

Page 57.

Here entreth the yere of o^r L. 1611.

The 18th of Aprill marryed John Ryddell & Alice Burdenson, wid.
The vijth of June marryed Arthure Whatman & Jane Goose.
The vijth of Octob^r marryed Willim Shroubsell & Susan Harding.
The same Day marryed Henrye Athorn & Dennis Maxsted.
The 4th of Nouemb̃^r mar. Richard Clyfford & Joan Meere.
The same Day marryed Austen Carr & Marie Hannington.
The 18th of Nouemb^r marryed John Edwards & Alice Turner.
The 20th of Januarie mar. Nicholas Juce & Joan Goose.
The 3^d of ffeb were mar. Mathew Packnam & Joan Downe.
The xvth of feb mar. Henrye Bayly & Phebe Charlton.

thus far certifyed.

1612 1612.

The vth of May marryed Mathew Abram & Margaret Dane.
The vth of May marryed John Andrewes & Elizabeth Juce.
The 18th of Januarie marryed Tobyas Bedle & Elizabeth Loue, widowe.

Anno Dom 1613.

The 4th of May Marryed John Haukes and Jane Day.
The 27th of Septemb^r marryed John Chawker and Lettice Waker.
The 22th of November marryed Lawrance Juice & Mary Tylsonne.
The 7th of ffebruarie maryed Leonard Meare and Rebca Goulson.

Heare entereth the yeare of o^r Lord 1614.

The 23th day of May marryed John Baker and Martha Juice.
The 20th daie of June marryed William Dane and Susan Browne.
The 18th Daye of July weare maried Thõs Renonles & Anne Tayler in Juuina L.
The 7th of August weare maried Robert ffissher and Christien Browninge.
The 3th of October were maried Edward Crathon and Johane Rayner.
The 10th of October wer maried Elias Boate & Alice Adams.
The 24th of October weare maried Richard Williams and Añe Denchley.
The 9th Day of January weare maried Ralph Walbancke & Margaret Bray.
The 23th of Januarie wer maryed Mathew Poope and Sara Bayley.
The same Day wer maried Mathew Scott & Tomsen Spencer.

Thus fare certifith.

Heare entereth 1615.

The 11th of December were maried John Nester and Bennet Hendman, both single.
The 22th daie of the same wer maried John Ball & Marie Brome.

Thus fare directlie sett Downe.

Page 58.

Here entreth the yeare of our Lord 1616.

Here entreth the yeare of Lord 1616.

The 8th daie of Apprill were maried William Tayler & Bennett Wilde.

The 25th of the same were maried Daniell Marshall & Hester Boate.

The 20th of June were maried John Mockett & Ann Williams, widowe.

The 8th daie of July was maried Thomas Scott & Patience Goulding.

The 9th of the same wer maried John Pittell & Marie Juice.

The 17th daie of September wer maried Caleb Heeler & Ursula ffearne.

The 14th daie of October were maried Barnabee Causey and Elizabeth Hills.

The 5th of November were maried Richard Maxted & Martha Avice.

The same day were maried Henry Shrubsole & Elizabeth Shrubsole.

The 11th of the same were maried James Whatman & Marie Travice.

The 14th day of January were maryed Stephan Pimb & Joane Wisse, widow.

Here entreth the yeare of our Lord 1617.

The 28th of Aprill were maried Thomas Maybācke & An Kidwell.

The 12th of Maye wer maried Thomas Hobbs & Joane Wetherley, widowe.

The third of June were maryed Ezechiell Maxted & Susan Maxted.

The last day of June were maryed Henry Athourne & An Essex, singlewoman.

The 22th of September were maryede Thomas Crepedy & Gillān Day, wid.

The 20th day of October were maryed John Gates & Meekenesse Juyce.

The 21^{ith} of the same were maryed William Mearse & Catherine Tibbals.

The 30th of the same were maried George Hilliard & Joane Terrett, *alias* Thomas, widdow.

The 8th day of Dēmber were maried Nicholas Haines & Ann Morecroste.

The 26th day of Januarie were maried John Rooke & Mary ffogg.

Page 59.

The 9th day of March wer maried John King and Jobane Haines, Singlewoman.

Here entreth ye yeare of o^r Lord 1618.

The 13th day of Aprill were maried George Halle and Elizabeth Tittell, widowe.

The first day of June were maried Richard Bensted thelder & Alice Snoode.

The 29th day of June were maried Robert Maxted and Mildred Hayward.

The 23th of Novemb^r maried Michaell Hilles and Joane Gouldsmith, wydowe.

The 14th of January maried Richard Anderson and Elizabeth Lewis.

Año Dom 1619:

The third of May wer maried Robert Baker & Margery Grigory.

The 25th of May wer maried Edward Bradford & Marie Enfield.

The last daie of May wer maried Wm Vicars and Alice Hilles.

The 15th of November wer maryed Richard Wood and Elizabeth Tilghmã.

The 16th day of November were maryed John Mashe and Avice Marshall.

The 14th of January were maryed Willam Conawaye and Joane Lewies.

The 28th day of ffebruarie were maryed Jehugh Johnson & Elizabeth Boate.

1620.

The 27th of July were maried Thomas Johnsonne and Joanne Terry of Throwley, widdowe.

The last day of July were mary Williã Crupe and Mary Pordage.

Her entreth the yeare of Lord 1621.

The 25th day of May were maryed William Chamberlen and Mary Place.

The 18th day of October were maried Nicholas Baker & Johane Todd.

The 31th day Octob^r were maried Thomas Howis & Margaret Baker.

The 4th day of Decemb^r were maryed Walter Baker of Kingdowne & Mary Claget of the Cittie of Cantbury.

The 17th day of June were maryed William Quoyfe and Mildred Maxted, widowe.

1622   1622   1622.

The 3th day of October wer maryed James Place and Elizabeth Brodstreet.

The 28th day of Nouemb^r were maryed John Nockes & Ellen Gilles.

The 20th day of January were Maryed Thomas Bynge and Namie Rankorne.

The 27th day of January were maried Thomas Day & Anne Hicks.

1623   1623   1623.

The 20th of August married Thomas Periman & Alice Boate, wid.

The 6th of Nouember were married John Giles & Catharine Rider.

The 24th of Nouember were married Nicholas Shroubsoll and Ann Hills.

The 9th of feb. were marryed Richard fryth & Catharine Gruve.

Page 60.   1624   1624.

The 27th day of May was married Mathew Hittell & Alice Kent.

The 29th day of July was married John Wengat & Ann Woodwall.

The sixt of Nouember married John Bush and Elizabeth Juce.

The 15 day of Nouember was maried William tayler and Elizabethe Ran .˙. .

The 18 of Nouember was maried Edman abram and Bennet ballden.

The 21 of December was maried Edward abram and Ami Pecknam.

the 10 of Januari was maried Nicolas frith and Catheren Grinstret.

The 3 of feuerari was maried Nicolas Shrubsol and Catheren foman.

The 14 of march was maried Thomas Leger and Elisabeth Place.

1625.

The 13th of Jun was John brooke and thomsin triben married 1625 1625.

the 19th of July was married william meerr and thomsin lewes.

the 30th of July was married nicolas fayerman and thomsin tutten.

the 13th of October wer married william howes and Allice Place.

the 24th of October weare maried William hanington and Cateren frith, wido.

the first of nouember wear maried John Doun and Sarah harison.

the 24th of nouember weare married John abram and phillis marth, wido.

1626   1626.

the 17th of apell was married Randall ludsom and Margree beckly.

the sam day was married Austen Carre and mary lewes, wido.

the fifteenthe of May weare married John Ewell and thomsin Spencer.

the 16th of January wear married John Call and Elisabeth mount.

by me PETTER PLACE
Amen annodommony the
Ragu of our King 1630.

Page 61 [*blank, only half a page*].

Page 62 [*only half a page*].

Mdñ that upon the ixth of August 1632 was grãted a licence to Dame Élizab: Routh wife of Sir John Routh of this pish in respect of her sicknesse & bodilie infirmitie to eat flesh according to a statute made to that purpose in quinto Elizabethe.

Page 63 [*blank*].

Page 64 [*blank*].

F

Page 65.   BURIALS.

Here beginnethe the yere of our Lord 1558.

The first of Aprill was buried Joan Edwards.

The xiiij^th of May was buried Philipp Burnell.

The xix^th of June was buried John Okenfold.

The 7th of Julye was buried Roƀt Juce.

The 26th of Julye was buried Rose Blackamoor.

The 3i^th of Julye was buried Blance Briston.

The i8^th of August was buried W^m ffennett.

The 6th of Septemƀ was buried Marie Pettit.

The same Daie was buried John Anker.

The xij of Septẽber was buried Stephan, a strang^r.

The 20th of Octoƀ was buried John Preston.

The 24th of Octoƀ was buried John Pane.

The xxvij of Octoƀ was buried John Juce.

The xiij^th of Nouẽb^r was buried Richard, a stranger.

The 24th of Decẽbr was buried John Shroubsoll.

The xxix^th of Decẽb^r was buried Hamon Shroubsoll.

The iii^th of Januarie was buried John Gyoll.

The 6th of Januarie was buried John Juce.

The first of Jan. was buried John Joanes.

The 20th of Jañarie was buried Arnold Pemble.

The xxj^th of Jan. was buried Ralf . . .

The same Daie was buried Alice Okenfold.

The 27th of Januarie was buried John Juce.

The 28th of Januarie was buried Joane Joanes.

The iij^d of ffeƀ was buried Adam Ceton.

The same Day was buried John Carter.

The iiij^th of ffeƀ was Buried Alice Gyall.

The xth of ffeƀ was buried Margaret Nispod.

The xi^th of ffeƀ was buried Willm Wilcocke.

The xij^th of feƀ was buried John Hoode.

The xiij^th of feƀ was buried Rabith Ceton.

The xiiij^th of feƀ was buried Margaret Raynerd.

The i8^th of feƀ was buried John . . .

The xix^th of ffeƀ wrs buried Margerie Shroubsoll.

The xxj^th of ffeƀ was buried Marion . . .

The vth of March was buried Raynold Smyth.

The ix^th of March was buried Thomas Dod.

The 14th of March was buried Jssabell Plummer.

The 15th of March was buried Henrie Chorteose.

1559.   Here eutreth the yere of our Lord 1559.

The xxix^th of March was buried Marion Norman.

The same Daie was buried Elliener Edwards.

The xv^th of Aprill was buried Henrie Shroubsoll.

The 2^d of May was buried Marg. Cytnall.

The same Day was buried Joan ffarnam.

The first of June was buried Thomas Blackborne.
The xvj^th of Julye was buried Marg. Okenfold.
The 21th of Julye was buried John Juce.
The iiij^th of Septeb^r was buried Edward Bruke.
The 8th of Septeb^r was buried John Marshall.
The xv^th of Octob^r was buried James Spycer.
The vth of Nouëb^r was buried Thomas Porredg.
The 17th of Decëb^r was buried Wm Place.
The 26th of Decëb^r was buried Elizabeth Goddard.
The xij^th of Januarie was buried Thomas Juce.

WILLIAM PLACE.
RICHARD RUCKE.
THOMAS HENDMAN. ⊕

Page 66.
The xij^th of Januarie was buried . . . Bere.
The vij^th of March was buried Rob̄t Bratt.

1560. Here entreth the yere of our Lord 1560.
The third of June was buried Joan Best.
The ix^th of June was buried Alice Rayner theld^r.
The xxij^th of June was buried John ffairebarne.
The vij^th of July was buried Alice Rayner infant.
The xvij^th of August was buried Ralf . . .
The xviij^th of Nouember was buried John Tennaker.
The 25th of Decëb^r was buried John Constable a stranger.
The xxi^th of Januarie was buried Margaret Brooke.
The iv^th of Jan. was buried Elizabeth Porredg the wyfe of Wm Porredg.
The 22th of ffeb. buried Thomas Hãmond.

1561. Here entreth the yere of our Lord 1561.
The xx^th of June was buried Margerie Best.
The xviij^th of August was buried Joan Burnell the wyfe of Thomas Burnell.
The xth of Septëb. was buried Margaret Ward.
The xxvi^th of Septëb^r was buried Joan Dunkyn.
The same Day was buried Dennis Par.
The xv^th of Octob̄ was buried Wiłłm Snell.
The xxiij^th of Nouëber was buried Edward Gayton.
The xxiij^th of Januarie was buried Joan Songer.
The 23th of feb was buried Joan Howlet *alias* Hamond.
The xx^th of ffeb̄ was buried . . . Denslake ye the wyfe of Christopher Denslake.
The xxvij^th of ffeb̄ was buried Thomas Rider.
The first of March . . . Pemerton, wid.
The xxj^th of March was buried Georg Hills.

1562. Here entreth the yere of our Lord 1562.
The xvij^th of May was buried Rob̄t Tom̄es a strang^r.
The xv^th of Septëb^r was buried Margaret Shroubsell the wyfe of Rychard Shroubsell theldest.

F²

The 17th of October was buried Agnes Brooke.
The xxixth of Octob^r was buried Joan Vicars.
The xth of Nouēb^r was buried Mathew Raynard.
The xijth of Nouēb^r was buried Parnell Bayley.
The xvth of Nouēb^r was buried fflorence Throwley.
The xjth of Nouēb^r was buried Elizabeth Bowyer.
The sixt of Decēb^r was buried Joan Gaten.
The vijth of Decēb^r was buried Alice Hammon.
The xvth of Decēb^r was buried Edmund Edlaye.
The xxth of Decēb^r was buried Jssabell Allen.
The xxiij of Decēb^r was buried Julian Preston.

1563. Here entreth the yere of our Lord 1563.

The last Daie of March was buried Elizab : Juce.
The xijth of Aprill was buried Thomas Burnell.
The xxiijth of Aprill was buried Heur. littleburie.
The xxviijth of Aprill was buried Joan Weldishe the wyfe of James Weldish.
The xxth of May was buried a strang Boy.
The iiijth of June was buried Adam Gyall.
The xiijth of June was buried Henrie Gaert.
The xxviijth of Julye was buried John . . .
The iij^d of August was buried John Pemsey.
The 7th of August was buried Thomas Porredg.
The 17th of Septēb^r was buried John Lull.
The 24th of Septēb^r was buried Joan Haṁon.
The sixt of Octob^r was buried Joan Powell.
The xvith of Octob^r was buried Marg Laurence.
The sixt of Nouēb^r was buried William . . .

WILLIAM PLACE.
RICHARD RUCKE.
THO : HENDMAN. ⊕

Page 67.

The 17th of Nouēb^r was buried Stephā Throwley.
The xxviijth of Nouēb^r was buried John Throwley The sonne of Thomas Throwley.
The xvith of Januar. was buried Alexand^r Grimsell.
The xxiijth of Jan. was buried Elizab : Bassocke.
The 24th of Januarie was buried Elisab : Dod.
The xvth of March was buried John Owen.
The 23th of March was buried Alice Bowcher.

1564. Here entreth the yere of our Lord 1564.

The first of Aprill was buried Agnes Burton.
The xiijth of May was buried Richard Paramour.
The 19th day of May was buried Alice Essex.
The 5th of June was buried Daniell Tylman.

The 17th of June was buried florence Jacob.
The xvijth of Septĕb^r was buried Marg. Brooke the Daught^r of Richard Brooke.
The 24th of Octob^r was buried Alice Porredge.
The 17th of Nouĕb^r was buried John Scott.
The 24th of Jan. was buried Joan Tyrrey.
The xxvjth of Jan. was buried Ann Throwley the Daught^r of Thomas Throwley.
The same Day was buried Rychard Adie the sonne of Rychard Adie.
The xith of March was buried Tho : Boche^r.

1565. Here entreth the yere of our Lord 1565.

The 25th of March was buried Ann Adie the Daughter of Rychard Adie.
The 8th Daie of May was buried Christo : Pramour.
The 28th of May was buried Jo : Best.
The 25th of June was buried Edward Lawrence the sonne of Wm Laurence.
The xxixth of Septĕbr Richard, a strãg^r.
The xth of Octob was buried Myldred Tylman.
The vith of Nouĕb^r was Wiłłm Juce, sen.
The iiijth of Jan. was buried Thomas Bulleye.
The 26th of Jan. was buried Edward ffocoler.
The 30th of Jan. was buried John Mosse.
The 20th of ffeb was buried John May.
The 26th of ffeb was buried Wm Collens.
The 28th of feb was buried James Tennaker.

1566. Here entreth the yere of our Lord 1566.

The xxth of March was buried John Dunkyn.
The xxixth of March was buried Marg : Dŭkyn.
The iiijth of Aprill was buried Philip a strang.
The xth of May was buried Marie Tennaker the wyfe of John Tennaker thelder.
The xxiijth of May was buried Joan Ellis.
The xth of June was buried . . . Hunt.
The xiiijth of Julye was buried Elizab : Brodstret.
The 3ith of August was buried Avis Clyfford.
The 20th of Septeb was buried Rose Allen.
The 6th of Jan. was buried John ffynn.
The xxth of Jan. was buried John Collens.
The xxiijth of Jan. was buried . . . Wylls.

WILLIAM PLACE.
RICHARD RUCK.
THOMAS HENDMAN. ⊕

Page 68.

The thrid of ffeb was buried Ellenor Place the Daughter of Ralf Place.
The xth of ffeb was buried Richard Norman.

The xxiij[th] of March buried from the white a maid, being a stranger.
The xxiiij of March was buried Wiłłm Laurence.

1567.   Here entreth the yere of our Lord 1567.

The 6th of Aprill was buried the Daughter of Michaell Hanning, A child.
The 6th of June was buried Wiłłm Best.
The ix[th] of June was buried Edward Hammon.
The xi[th] of June was buried Joan Collens.
The 6th of Julye was buried Henrie Channell.
The 6th of August was buried Susan Shroubsell, the Daught[r] of Richard Shroubsoll.
The 7th of August was buried Joan Cooper the wyfe of John Cooper.
The xviiij[th] of Noueb[r] was buried Arthur Porredge.
The 6 of Deceb[r] was buried Avis Shroubsoll.
The iij[th] of Jan. was buried Joan Edwards, Wid.
The 21th of March was buried Christop[r] Haukes.
The 22th of March was buried Joan Shroubsoll.

1568.   Here entreth the yere of our Lud 1568.

The first of Aprill was buried florence Pettyt, the wyfe of Cirriaek Pettyt, esquire.
The xviij[th] of Aprill was buried Mabell Place.
The 27th of Aprill was buried Thomas Ellis.
The 12th of Julye was buried Wiłłm Pettyt.
The 7th of Septeb[r] was buried John Bryer.
The xxvi[th] of Sept. was buried Luce, a strang[r].
The same Daie was buried Elizab: Brodstrete.
The 4th of Noueb[r] was buried Tomsyn Wylls.
The xth of Noueb[r] was buried Wiłłm folye.
The 26th of Noueb[r] was buried John Wylls.
The xiiij[th] of Deceb[r] was buried Tho: Wiggall.
The xx[th] of Janu. was buried Marie Thomson.
The xv[th] of ffeb was buried Catharin Constable.
The 2[d] of March was buried Marie Dunkyn.

1569.   Here entreth the year of our Lud 1569.

The xxiij[th] of Aprill was buried Edward Kyng.
The first of May was buried W[m] Brockwoll.
The 18th of May was buried Elizabeth Percivall.
The 20th of May was buried John Shroubsoll.
The 24th of July was buried John Pope.
The 22th of Octob was buried Edward Pettyt.
The 29th of Octob was buried Alice Warden.
The xth of Decemb was buried urselley, the child of a stranger.
The ix[th] of Januarie was buried Marg. Essex.
The 5th of March buried Alice Belke.

1570. Here entrethe the yer of our Lud i570.
The 6th of June was buried Elizabeth Juce, wid.
The second of Julye was buried John Golson.
The xth of August was buried Margaret Dickson.

WILLIAM PLACE.
RICHARD RUCK
THOMAS HENDMAN. ⊕

Page 69.
The 6th of Septeb was buried Elizabeth Mount.
The first of Octob was buried Richard Adie.
The vth of Decemb was buried Avis Allen.
The 8th of Januarie was buried Elizab : Burnell.

Here endeth the old Register. All the Burialls from the 8th of Januarie i570 to the xix of Nouember i57i are wantinge, and ar not to be found in our church bookes.

1571. Here eutreth the yere of our Lud i57i.
The xxth of Nouëbr was buried Richard Gyll a stranger.
The 30th of Nouëbr buried Margaret Johnson.
The 2d of Decëbr was buried Christopr Denslake.
The 8th of Decëbr was buried Wiłłm Hammon.
The xij of Januar. was buried Cirilla Grimsell, widow.
The xvth of Jan. buried Nicholas . . .

1572. Here entrethe the yere of our Lud i572.
The 25th of March was buried Susan Blanket.
The 14th of May was buried Steven Paramour.
The ixth of Julye was buried Marie Burnell.
The 18th of August was buried Alice Pecknam.
The 22th of Septëbr was buried Edw : Clyfford.
The 9th of Octobr was buried John Lye.
The xxth of Nouëbr was buried a stranger.
The viljth of Decëbr was buried Joan Maxsted.
The xxvijth of Decëbr was buried Joan Preston.
The first of feb was buried Wiłłm Shroubsoll.
The xth of feb was buried Joan Hammon.
The 26th of feb was buried Edward Dunkyn.
The xviijth of feb was buried Elizabeth Hunt.
The 2d of March was buried Dorothie Ore.
The 6th of March was buried Georg Knepe.
The 13th of March was buried Tomsyn Bartlett.

1573. Here entreth the yere of our Lord 1573.
The 2d of Aprill was buried Stephan Shroubsoll.
The 30th of Aprill was buried Tomsyn Tennaker.

The 7th of May was buried Christopher Shroubsoll.
The xxth of May was buried Joan Patinson.
The xijth of Septēbr was buried Robert Eyre esquire.
The 3th of Nouēbr was buried Dennis Halloway.
The first of Octobr was buried John Rucke.
The ixth of Decēbr was buried Wiłłm Blunkett.
The 28th of Januarie was buried John Coxe.
The 31th of Jan. was buried Margaret Crekes.
The 22th of feb was buried Timothie Martyn.
The iijth of March was buried Elizabeth Gyll.
The 27th of March was buried John Cooper.

thus far exhibited to the ordinarie.

1574.   Here entreth the yere of our Lord 1574.

The 21th of May was buried Henrie Hammon.
The 19th of June was buried Stephan Wyman.
The 23th of June was buried Rychard Bowne.
The 23th of Julye was buried Georg Kenytt.
The jth of August was buried John Page, base borne.
The 20th of Septēbr was buried John ffreind.
The same Daie was buried Cyrilla Cocke.
The 6th of Octob was buried Joan Wyman.

WILLIAM PLACE.
RICHARD RUCKE.
THOMAS HENDMAN. ⊕

Page 70.

The 6th of Octobr was buried Cathar : Shroubsoll.
The 25th of Octobr was buried Ann Shroubsoll.
The viijth of Nouēbr was buried Susan Shroubsoll.
The 2d of Nouēbr Ann Ore, the wyfe of Andrew Ore.
The 7th of Decēbr was buryed Ralf Gruddall.
The xvth of Decēbr was buried Thomas . . .
The 18th of Decēbr was buried Stephan Allen, the sonne of Nicholas Allyn.
The 28th of Decēbr was buried a woman, a stranger.
The 17th of feb was buried Robert Abram.
The 24th of feb was buried Elizabeth Pensey, Widow.
The 18th of March was buried John Presson.

1575.   Here entreth the yere of our Lord 1575.

The 2d of Aprill was buried John Pollard the sonne of Edward Pollard.
The 25th of Aprill was buried Joan Abram, Wid.
The 6th of May was buried Margarie Bayley, the wyfe of John Bayley.
The 7th of May was buried John Gest, a child.
The xvth of May was buried Stepħa Shroubsoll.
The 5th of June was buried Rychard Porredg, the sonne of Stephan Porredge.

The 5th of Septẽbr was buried Edmund Abram.

The 19th of Septẽbr was buried John Cornish, a base borne child.

The xxjth of Nouẽbr was buried Robert Tompson, vicar of this prish.

The xiiijth of feb was buried A man, a stranger.

The xixth of feb was buried Ellen Rowland, the Daughter of Rychard Rowland.

The xvjth of March was buried John Austen.

1576. Here entreth the yere of our L. 1576.

The last of March was buried a woman, a stranger, whose name we know not.

The i4th of Aprill was buried Thomas Kynge.

The xiij of May was buried Margaret Maxsted the wyfe of Robert Maxsted.

The 28th of June was buried John fryar the sonne of John ffryar.

The i8th of Julye was buried a strange Boy that was found dead at the Parsonage.

The 20th of Julye was buried Alice Bensted the wife of Stephan Bensted.

The 26th of Nouẽbr was buried Marie Haukyns the Daughtr of Tho: Haukyns the youngr.

Thus far certified the 27th of Nouember.

The io th of Decẽbr was buried Edmond Raynolds.

The i6th of feb was buried Elizabeth Browne.

The i8th of feb was buried Dennis Maxsted.

The 2ith of feb was buried Michaell Dylet.

Here entreth ye yere of our L. 1577. 1577.

The iiij of Aprill was buried Nicholas Allen.

The 8th of Aprill was buried John ffairman.

The i4th of Aprill was buried John Jacob the son of Mathie Jacob.

WILLIAM PLACE.
RICHARD RUCKE.
THOMAS HENDMAN. ⊕

Page 71.

The 2ith of Aprill was buried Mathew Balden the sonne of John Balden.

The 6th of May was buried Thomas Uprichard.

The i4th of May was buried Elizabeth Pargate.

The 4th of June was buried Ann Shroubsoll.

The 2th of August was buried Ann Shroubsoll.

The 8th of August was buried Wm Hussye.

The 20th of Septẽbr was buried Susan Maxsted.

The 22th of Septẽbr was buried Alice Chillenden.

The i6th of Octob was buried Richard Norman.

The 26th of Octob was buried Alice Hussye.

The 26th of Decẽbr was buried Richard Carter.

The 11th of Januarie was buried Math: Spencer.

The 20th of March buried Elizabeth Carter.

1578. Here entreth the yere of our L. 1578.

The 8th of June was buried Elizabeth Turner.
The 8th of August was buried Ellenor Abram.
The 10th of August was buried Marg. Carr.
The 14th of Septeb^r was bur^d Elizabeth Maxsted.
The 22th of Septr was buried A poore man a stranger.
The 28th of Septeb^r was bur^d Willm. Dunkyn.
The 8th of Noueb^r was buried Margaret Wiles.
The 20th of Noueb^r was bur^d Tomsyn Baylei.
The 21th of Deceb^r wae bur^d Margaret ffryar.
The 9th of feb was buried Joan Cooper.
The 11th of feb was buried Marke Croyden.

1579. Here entreth the yere of our L. 1579.

The 15th of Aprill was bur^d John Shroubsoll.
The 18th of June was buried Dennis Kynge.
The 30th of June was buried Susan Shroubsol.
The 9th of Julie was buried Tomsyn Ellis.
The 4th of August was bur. John Hussye.
The 22th of August was buri^d John Abraham.
The 29th of August was buried Thomas Dine.
The first of Septeb^r was bur^d John Carr.
The 15th of Nouember was buried the worshipfull Elizabeth Eyre, wid.
The 29th of feb was buried Dennis Kesten.
The 2^d of March was bur^d Robert Treppling.
The 11th of March was buried John Rucke.
The 15th of March was buried Henrie Bucke.

Here entrethe the yere of our L. 1580.

The 18th of Aprill was bur. Ann Moore.
The 8th of May was buried ffaith Jackson.
The 23th of May was bur^d Thomas Marshall.
The 11th of June was bur^d Rychard Bradford.
The 13th of June was bur. Margaret Clyfford.
The 4th of Julye was buried Ann Cornish.
The 20th of Julye was buried Johan Barns.
The 24th of July was bur^d Jane Littlewood.
The 5th of August was bur^d Thomas Brice.
The first of Octob^r was bur^d Jane Golson.

WILLIAM PLACE.
RICHARD RUCKE.
THOMAS HENDMAN. ⊕

Page 72.

The 9th of October was buried Henrie Okenfold.
The 17th of Octob^r was buried Venicon Goodyn.
The 22th of Octob^r was buried Laurence Martyn.
The 24th of Noueb^r was buried Christopher Rucke.
The 30th of December was buried Joan Croyden.

The first of March was bur. Martha Pyrkyn.
The 7th of March was bur. Henrie Pettyt.
The 8th of March was buried Raynold Turner.

1581.   Here entrethe the yere of our L. 1581.
The 18th of Aprill was buried Abraham Scott.
The 21th of Aprill was buried Marie Raynolds.
The 14th of May was buried Ann Dūkyn.
The 20 and 22th of June were bur^d Thomas and Wiłłm Keeler.
The 26th of Septēb^r was bur^d Agnes Rucke.
The 9th of Octob^r was bur^d John Bayley.
The 30th of Octob^r was buried Joan Bucke.
The 9th of Januarie was buried Henrie Kersbye.
The 3^d of March was buried Ann Balden.
The 11th of March was buried Mathie Brett.

1582.   Here entreth the yere of our L. 1582.
The 15th of Aprill was buried Thomas Kyng.
The 26th of Aprill was buried Joan Dine.
The 27th of Aprill was buried Joan Throwley.
The 11th of May was bur^d Richard Shroubsoll.
The 30th of May was buried John Tennaker.
The 5th of Julie was bur^d Wiłłm flud.
The 12th of Julie was bur^d Joan Saukyn.
The 29th of Julie was buried Susan Hussye.
The 7th of Septēbr was buried John Nox.
The 20th of Septēb^r was bur^d Marg^t Denslake.
The 5th of Nouēber was bur^d Joan Dunkyn.
The 12th of Nouēb^r was buried William Norman.
The 13th of Nouēb^r was bur^d Stephan Norman.
The 23th of Nouēb^r was bur^d Dorothie Goodchild.
The 26th of Nouēb^r was buried Andrewe Perkyn,
The 22th of Decēb^r was bur^d John Abram.
The 25th of Decēb^r was bur^d John Woodwall.
The 5th of Januarie was buried . . . Perkyn.
The 15th of feb was buried Marie Pettyt.

1583.   Here entreth the yere of our L. 1583.
The 27th of March was buried Marie Dine.
The 8th of Julie was buried John Browne.
The 29th of Julie was buried John Brigen.
The 22th of August was bur^d Peter Raynolds.
The 6th of Octob was buried Luce Bayley.
The 20th of Nouember were buried John and Isack Chillenden.
The 21th of Nouēb^r was buried Henrie Tyler.
The 14th of Januarie was bur. Tho : Holland.
The 23th of Janū was bur. Nicholas Roger.
The 24th of Jan. was bur. Rychard, a stranger.

The 26th of Jan. was bur^d Alice Roger.
The 6th of feb was bur^d Paule Bucke.
The 11th of feb. was bur^d Brooke.
The 13th of feb. was bur^d John Raynold.

WILLIAM PLACE.
RICHARD RUCKE.
THOMAS HENDMAN. ⊕

Page 73.
The 22th of feb was buried John Browne.
The 23th of feb was bur. John Turner.
The same Daie was buried Thomas Barnell.
The 27th of feb was buried Ann Brooke.
The 9th of March was bur^d William Brown.
The 15th of March was bur. Robert Brooke.

1584. Here entreth the yere of our L. 1584.
The 7th of Aprill was bur^d Agnes farnam.
The same Daie was buried Willm Jefferry.
The 19th of Aprill was buried Thomas a strange^r.
The 19th of June was buried Joan Kynge.
The 3^d of Julie was bur^d . . . Chillenden.
The 25th of August was bur. Richard Spring a stranger.
The 26th of August was buried . . . Jdden.
The 28th of August was buried Marie ffludd.
Certified the 18th of Octob^r 1584.

The 21th of Octob. was bur^d Mathie Howesse.
The 22th of Octr was buried Robert Joanes.
The 29th of Octob. was buried Parnell Pollard.
The 11th of Noucb. was bur. Joan Collen.
The 28th of Jan. was bur^d Mildred Collen.

1585. Here entreth the yere of our L. 1585.
The 7th of Aprill was bur. Priscilla Haukins.
The 13th of Aprill was bur^d Alice Raynolds.
The 28th of Aprill was bur^d Robert Maxsted.
The 13th of May was buried John ffryar.
The 30th of June was bur. Jonas Howesse.
The 18th of Septeb^r was bur. William Teñaker.
The 23th of Octob^r was bur^d Agnes Shroubsoll.
The 5th of Deceb^r was buried Willm Hills.
The 14th of Januarie was bur^d Henrie Lambe.
The 25th of Jan. was buried Hugh A Powell.
The 15th of feb was bur^d Joan Blunkett.
The 21th of feb was bur^d John . . ., a stranger.
The 23th of feb was bur^d Agnes Hamon.

1586. Here entreth the yere of our L. 1586.

The 10th of May was bur. Margaret Rayner.
The 27th of May was burd Margaret . . .
The 18th of June was burd Thomas Bayley.
The 17th of Julie was bur. Richard Todd.
The 24th of Julie was bur. Ann Chillenden.
The 28th of August was bur. Wm. Clyfford.
The 17th of Septẽbr was bur. Richard Juce.
The 18th of Septr burd Elizabeth Swann.
The 6th of Octobr was burd Hew, a stranger.
The 17th of Decẽbr was burd William Jackson.
The 24th of March was burd Alice Edwards.

1587. Here entreth the yere of our L. 1587.

The 15th of May was buried Albert Bassett, Vicar of this Prish.
The first of Julie was burd Edward Howesse.
The 20th of Julie was burd Elizabeth Hills.
The 26th of Augt was bur. Gabriell Hills, infans.
The 3d of Septẽbr was burd Joan Blunkett, infans.
The 9th of Septẽbr was burd William Todd.

> WILLIAM PLACE.
> RICHARD RUCKE.
> THOMAS HENDMAN. ⊕

Page 74.

The xith of Septembr was burd Margaret Scot.
The 20th of Septẽbr was burd Elizabeth Snoth.
The 24th of Septẽbr was burd John Ellis.
The 21th of Octobr was buried Mathew Haukyns.
The 11th of Nouẽbr was buried Alice Cornishe, the wyfe of Philipp Cornishe.
The 16th of Nouẽbr was buried Brigett Hanning, the wyfe of Nicholas Hanning.
The 6th of Decembr was buried Bennet, the wyfe of John Goodden.
The 18th of Decẽbr was burd Nicholas Hanning.
The 30th of Decẽber was burd Simon Abram, the sonn of Raynold Abram, infans.
The 29th of feb was buried Willyam Hills.
The 20th of March was buried Thomas Haukyns, thelder, houshr.

Thus far certified to the ordinarie.

1588. Here entreth the yere of our L. 1588.

The 18th of Aprill was bur. John Rogers.
The 22th of Aprill was burd a gerle of Cornishs.
The xiijth of Julie was bur. a poore man, a stranger.
The 3d of August was buried Andrew Ower.
The 7th of Septẽber was buried Tobias Scott, the son of Mathew Scott, puer.

The 22ᵗʰ of Septēber was burᵈ Ann Berry svant.
The i8ᵗʰ of Octobʳ was burᵈ a Crysomer of John Berryes.
The 27ᵗʰ of Octobʳ was buried a child of Thomas Downes.
The 30ᵗʰ of Octobʳ was burᵈ Davy Joanes housholdʳ.
The 17ᵗʰ of Nouēbeʳ was buried a Crysomer of Thomas Gooses.
The 23ᵗʰ of Nouēbʳ was burᵈ Alice Place, the elder.
The 24ᵗʰ of Nouēbʳ was burᵈ Mother Browne, wid.
The 27ᵗʰ of Nouēb was burᵈ Wiħm Place housholđ.
The 29ᵗʰ of Nouēb was burᵈ Alice Place, Jun.
The 8ᵗʰ of Decēb was burᵈ Ann Bucke, infans.
The 15ᵗʰ of December was burᵈ Arthure Whatman the son of James
    Whatman.
The first of Januarie was buried Mathew Vigars.
The 2iᵗʰ of Jan. burᵈ Philip Cornish.
The 23ᵗʰ of Januarie burᵈ the wife of John Blunket.
The xiijᵗʰ of feƀ was burᵈ Ralf Hart.
The xviijᵗʰ of feƀ was burᵈ Thomas Keeler the sonne of Thomas
    Keler, infans.

1589.   Here entreth the yere of our L. i589.

The 28ᵗʰ of March was burᵈ Edw : Pollard, housholdʳ.
The 23ᵗʰ of Aprill was buried Ann Kesten the wyfe of Thomas
    Kesten.
The i8ᵗʰ of May was buried Johan Litlewood the wyfe of Thomas
    Littlewood.
The 8ᵗʰ of Julie was bur : Georg Juse the son of Nicholas Juce, child.
The 25ᵗʰ of August was bur. John Carter the sonn of John Carter.

WILLIAM PLACE.
RICHARD RUCKE.
THOMAS HENDMAN. ⊕

Page 75.

The 28th of August was buried Elizabeth Hills, wid.
The i8ᵗʰ of Septēbʳ John Allen.

thus far certified.

The 26ᵗʰ of Decēbʳ was buried William Carr, the son of James Carr.
The 9ᵗʰ of Januarie was buried John Carr, the son of James Carr.
The 22ᵗʰ of Jan. was buried John Goodden.
The 29ᵗʰ of Jan. was bur. Thomas Howesse.
The 22ᵗʰ of Jan. was bur. the wyfe of Laurence.
The first of feƀ was buried Laurence Kyng.
The 3ᵈ of feƀ was bur. Nicholas Hañington.
The 6ᵗʰ of feƀ was bur. Ann Scott.
The 20ᵗʰ feƀ was bur. William Goose.
The 8ᵗʰ of March was bur. Thomas Brenn.
The 24ᵗʰ of March was bur. Wiħm Presson.

1590. Here entreth the yere of o^r L. 1590.

The 27th of March was bur. Ann Berrye, wid.

The 30th of March was bur. Bennet Hager.

The 30th of March was bur. Robt Shroubsoll, the son of William Shroubsoll.

The 26th of Aprill bur. Willm Trumper.

The 4th of May was bur. Mark Kyng, the son of Austen Kyng.

The 6th of May buried Alice ffyn, wid.

The 3^d of Septẽb^r was bur. Tho: Blunkett.

The 6th of Octob^r was buried Catharine Hendman, the Wyfe of Thomas Hendmã.

Thus far certified the 7th of Octob^r 1590.

The 26th of Octob^r bur. Marie Car, the Daughter of James Car, child.

The 5th of Nouẽb^r was buried Elizabeth Swan, daught^r of Stephã Swann.

The 6th of Decẽb^r was buried Roger Reue, senex.

The 20th of Decẽber was bur. Avery Gavyn.

The 5th of Jan. was bur. John Cadman, Juvenis.

The 7th of Jan. was buried Peregrin Smith, infans, the Daught^r of Ralf Smith, stranger.

The 4th of feb was bur^d poore man, a stranger.

The 7th of feb was bur^d Ofnell Scot, houshold^r.

The 10th of feb bur^d an old man, a stranger.

The 26th of feb was bur^d Edward Kyng the son of Austen Kyng.

1591. Here entreth the yere of our L. 1591.

The 25th of March bur. Catharine ffairmã, wid.

The first of Aprill was bur. Betteris Joans, wid.

The 16th of Aprill was bur. Catharine Bush the daught^r of Will. Bushe, child.

The 15th of Julie was buried Thomas Kyng the son of Christopher Kyng, child.

The 22th of July was bur. Jean Gray, child.

The 30th of Julie was bur. Susan Juce the wyfe of Edw : Juce.

WILLIAM PLACE.

RICHARD RUCK.

THOMAS HENDMAN. ⊕

Page 76.

The 27th of August was buryed Rychard Shroubsoll of Crouch, householder.

thus far certified the 28th of Septẽb^r 1591.

The 29th of Septeb^r was buried Gabriell Amytt, the son of Robert Amytt, child.

The 15th of Octob^r was buried Cirriacke Pettytt, Esquire, houshold^r.

The 26th of Octob^r was buried Rose Swan, the wyfe of Stephan Swan.

The third of Decẽb^r was buried Elizabeth Dryland, the wyfe of John Dryland, gent.

The 8ᵗʰ of Decẽbʳ was bur. John Blunket, the sonne of John Blunkett.
The 16ᵗʰ of Decẽbʳ was burᵈ Rychard ffarnam, senex.
The xiiij of Januarie was buried Christian Bucke, wid.
The 24ᵗʰ of feb was buried Sara Bucke, Daughter of James Bucke, child.
The 13ᵗʰ of feb was burᵈ one Drywer, a strangʳ.

1592. Here entreth the yere of our L. 1592.

The 26ᵗʰ of March was buryed Joan Dine, the wyfe of Edward Dine.
The last of March was buried Margaret Scot, Daughter of James Scot, child.
The 14ᵗʰ of Aprill was buried John Scott, the son of James Scott, child.
The 23ᵗʰ of Aprill bur. John Blůket houshold.
The 17ᵗʰ of May was buried Dorothie Pettyt, the Daughter of Henrie Pettyt, gent.
The 20ᵗʰ of May was buried Ann Hills, the Daughter of Georg Hills.
The 16ᵗʰ of May was buried Priscilla Chappell, the Daughtʳ of John Chappell.
The 24ᵗʰ of May was bur. John Knot, householdʳ.
The 10ᵗʰ of July bur. Ann Curtesse, wid., a strangʳ.
The 24ᵗʰ of Julye was buried Nicholas Wood the son of Wylliam Wood, infans.
The 27ᵗʰ of Septẽbʳ was buried Thomsyn Shroubsoll the wyfe of Wᵐ Shroubsoll.
The 28ᵗʰ of Septẽbʳ was bur. Thomsyn Shroubsoll the Daughtʳ of Willm Shroubsoll, infans.
The 28ᵗʰ of Septẽbʳ was buried Willm Cornish the son of Rychard Cornish, infans.

Thus far certified the 4ᵗʰ of Octobʳ 1592.

The 8ᵗʰ of Octobʳ was buried Julyã Harris, wid.
The xixᵗʰ of Octobʳ was bur. Wyllyam Rucke at the stile, householdʳ.
The 21ᵗʰ of Octobʳ was buried James Chappell the son of John Chappell, child.
The 24ᵗʰ of Octob. was buried Thomas ffynch son of William ffynch, gent.
The 25ᵗʰ of Octob. was buried Henrie Jacob the son of Mathie Jacob, puer.
The 10ᵗʰ of Nouẽber was buried John Spencer the son of John Spencer, Juvenis.
The 16ᵗʰ of Nouẽb. was buried Marie Juce the Daughter ot Nicholas Juce, infans.
The 18ᵗʰ of Nouẽmb. was buried Alice Kennard the wyfe of John Kennard.

WILLIAM PLACE.
RICHARD RUCKE.
THOMAS HENDMAN. ⊕

Page 77.

The 2i^th of December was buried John Chillenden of ffairebrook, houshold^r.

The 24th of Decēb^r was buried Elizabeth Maxsted, the wyfe of John Maxsted.

The same Daie was buried Susan Tad, the Daughter of Nicholas Tad, infans.

The 26th of Decēb^r was buried Ann Lye, wid.

The last of Decēb^r was buried Ann Kyng, the Daught^r of Thomas Kyng.

The 9th of Januarie was buried Rose Adie, wid.

The i8^th of Januarie was buried Thomas Johnson, Juuenis.

The 28th of Januarie was buried Ann Sharp, the wyfe of Robt Sharp.

The 4th of feb was buried Raynold Shroubsell, the son of Rychard Shroubsoll.

The 17th of feb was buried Susan Marshall, the wyfe of Mathew Marshall.

The i8^th of feb was buried Ann Dadson, the Daught^r of . . . Dadson, child.

The 22th of feb was buried William Broke, senex.

The 23th of feb was buried Nicholas Dowe, Juvenis.

The first of March was buried Thomas Kyng, household^r.

The 12th of March was buried John Berrye, housholder.

The 2i^th of March was buried Stephan Blunkett, Juuenis.

The 23th of March was buried Nathaniell Brooke, the son of Laurence Broke.

The i5^th of March was buried Wylliam Brooke the son of Laurence Broke, infans.

1593. Here entreth the yere of our L. 1593.

The 11th of Aprill was buried Andrew Croyden, household^r.

The 4th of May was buried Thomas Maxsted, the son of Robt Maxsted, child.

The 11th of May was buried Anne Keler, the Daught^r of Thomas Keler.

The 12th of June was buried Marie Rucke the Daught^r of Cirriack Rucke, child.

The 20th of June was buried Jean Lowe, the wyfe of Timothie Lowe.

The last of July was bur. a strang^r, a woman.

The 12th of August was bur. Willim a strang^r, child.

The 16th of August was buried Ellenor Powell & Elizabeth Scot, child.

The 26th of August was buried Catharine Bayley, wid.

The last of August was buried Elizabeth Hammon, puella.

The 4th of Septēb^r was buried John Cornish, householder.

WILLIAM PLACE.
RICHARD RUCKE.
THOMAS HENDMAN. ⊕

G

Page 78.

The 22ᵗʰ of Septĕbʳ was buried Alice Cornish, wid.

The s ne Daie was buried Jean Parke the Daughtʳ of Abraham Parks.

The 25ᵗʰ of Septĕbʳ was buried Thomas Rider the son of Daniell Rider, puer.

The 27ᵗʰ of Septĕbʳ was buried Mathie Jacob, housholder.

Thus far certified the 11ᵗʰ of Octobʳ 1593.

The 22ᵗʰ of Nouember was buried Bennet Hendman the wyfe of Thomas Hendman.

The 24ᵗʰ of Nouĕbʳ was buried James Scot, housholder.

The 18ᵗʰ of Decĕbʳ was buried Roƀt Kire.

The 21ᵗʰ of Decĕbʳ was buried Marie Turfree, baseborne child.

The 27ᵗʰ of Decĕbʳ was buried Ann Jdden the Daughter of Georg Jdden, child.

The 4ᵗʰ of Januarie was buried Joan Claygate the wyfe of John Claygate.

The 16ᵗʰ of Januarie was buried John Ansted the son of John Ansted, child.

The 24ᵗʰ of Januarie was buried Thomas Ellys, senex.

The 7ᵗʰ of feƀ was buryed John Tymm houshouldʳ.

The 3ᵈ of March buried Nicholas Shroubsoll houshouldʳ.

The 3ᵈ of March was buried Avis Shroubsoll the wyfe of Rychard Shroubsoll, houshouldʳ.

1594.   Here entreth the yere of our L. 1594.

The 28ᵗʰ of March was buried William Blankett of the towne of ffevʳsham, houshouldʳ.

The 18ᵗʰ of Aprill was buried Marie Cornish the Daughtʳ of Richard Cornish.

The 13ᵗʰ of May was buried Repentance called the son of Thomas Handley.

The 18ᵗʰ of Maie was buried Ann Pantrye the wyfe of Ralf Pantrye.

The 25ᵗʰ of Aprill was buried Edward Shroubsoll, senex, houshouldʳ.

The 15ᵗʰ of June was buried Susan Croyden, the Daughtʳ of Andrew Croyden, child.

The 22ᵗʰ of June was buried Ann Downe, the Daughter of Thomas Downe, child.

The 4ᵗʰ of Julye was buried Joan Keeler, the Daughter of Thomas Keler, child

The first of Septĕbʳ was buried John Whinder, a stranger from the Bull.

The 21ᵗʰ of Septĕbʳ was buried Rychard Tym, the son of John Tym, puer.

thus far certified the ixᵗʰ of Octobʳ 1594.

The 26ᵗʰ of Octobʳ was buried John Latt, houshod.

The 22ᵗʰ of Januarie was buried Alice Chillenden, the Daughtʳ of John Chillenden, child.

The 21ᵗʰ of Januarie was buried Edward Longley, housholder.
The 22ᵗʰ of feb was buried Ann Whatman, the Daughter of James Whatman, child.
The 3ᵈ of March was buried John Pope, the son of Thomas Pope.

1595. Here entreth the yere of our L. 1595.
The 13ᵗʰ of Aprill buried Rychard Shroubsoll, housholder.
The 27ᵗʰ of Aprill buried John Hewes.

WILLIAM PLACE.
RICHARD RUCKE.
THOMAS HENDMAN. ⊕

Page 79.

The 20ᵗʰ of Aprill was buried Tho : Littlewood, senex.
The 27ᵗʰ of Aprill was buried Hercules Hills, householder.
The 2ᵈ of May was buried Thomas Rucke, the son of James Rucke, child.
The 16ᵗʰ of May was buried Edward Tennaker, the son of Edward Tennaker.
The 19ᵗʰ of May was buried Sara Rayner, the Daughter of Samuel Rayner, child.
The 27ᵗʰ, of June was bur. Thomas Throwley, senex.
The 6ᵗʰ of June was bur. Henrie Joanes, housholdr.
The 16ᵗʰ of Julye was buried Avis Jacob, the Daughter of Cirriacke Jacob, child.
The 28ᵗʰ of August was buried Richard Bunker.
The 16ᵗʰ of Octobʳ was buried John, a stranger.
The 15ᵗʰ of Noūebʳ was buried Margaret Brooke, the wyfe of Laurence Brooke.
The 29ᵗʰ of Noūebʳ was buried Cirriack Jacob, the son of Cir. Jacob, child.
The 6ᵗʰ of Decēbʳ was buried William Wayfare, a stranger.
The 26ᵗʰ of December was buried John Reues, housholder.
The 14ᵗʰ of Januarie was buried Edmund Chillenden, the son of William Chillenden.
The 22ᵗʰ of Januarie was buried Water Jeffry, senex.
The 16ᵗʰ of March was buried Thomas Tennaker, son of Thomas Tennaker, Juuenis.

thus far certified the 2ᵈ Day of Aprill 1595.

1596. Here entreth the yere of our L. 1596.
The 6ᵗʰ of Aprill was buried William Terret the son of John Terret, child.
The 12ᵗʰ of Aprill was buried Stephan Bensteed, housholder.
The 28ᵗʰ of May was buried Robt Nox the son of John Nox, child.
The 28ᵗʰ of June was buried Thomas Pettyt the son of Henrie Pettit, gent : child.

G²

The 23ᵗʰ of Julye was buried ffrances Haukyns the son of Thomas Haukins, gent., child.

The 13ᵗʰ of August was buried Bennet Peerse, Daughtʳ of . . . Peerse, child.

thus far certified the 7ᵗʰ of Octobʳ 1596.

The 28ᵗʰ of Octobʳ was buried Daniell Rider, housholdʳ.

The 26ᵗʰ of Octobʳ was buried . . . fylcot the son of Willm ffylcot, child.

The 17ᵗʰ of Nouēbʳ was buried Nicholas Wood the sonne of Willm Wood, infans.

The 24ᵗʰ of Nouēbʳ was buried Tho: Brown, householder.

The 16ᵗʰ of December was bur. John Gardiner, Juuenis.

The 31ᵗʰ of Januarie was buried Thomas Maxsted son of Robt Maxsted, child.

The 12ᵗʰ of feb buried Ann Bellowes, servant.

> WILLIAM PLACE.
> RICHARD RUCKE.
> THOMAS HENDMAN. ⊕

Page 80.

The 13ᵗʰ of feb was buried Christopher Kyng, housholder.

The 16ᵗʰ of feb was buried A poore Boy, a stranger that died at the Bull.

The 16ᵗʰ of March was buried John Kennard son of John Kennard, child.

The 21ᵗʰ of March was buried Catharine Pope the wyfe of Thomas Pope.

The 23ᵗʰ of March was buried Joan Shroubsell, widow.

1597.   Here entrethe the yere of our L. 1597.

The 3ᵈ of Aprill was buried Willm Juce, senex, householder.

The 21ᵗʰ of Aprill was buried Paule Spencer, housholdʳ.

The 5ᵗʰ of May was buried Christopher Allen the son of Robert Allen.

The 10ᵗʰ of May was buried Ann Golson the wife of John Golson.

The 13ᵗʰ of May was buried John Martyn, housholdʳ.

The 18ᵗʰ of May was buried Joan Cornish the wife of Willm Cornish.

The 25ᵗʰ of May was buried Ann Cornish the wyfe of Laurence Cornish.

The same day was buried Elizabeth Pantry the Daughter of Ralf Pantry, infans.

The 29ᵗʰ of May was buried Margerie Spencer the wid. of Paule Spencer.

The 29ᵗʰ of June was buried John Goose the son of Thomas Goose, child.

The 21ᵗʰ of Julye was buried Robt Jeffrye of Stapleherst, housholdʳ,

thus far certified the 11ᵗʰ of Octobʳ 1597.

The 2^d of Octob^r was buried Edward fylcot the son of William fylcot, infans.

The first of Janu. was buried Thomas Shroubsell son of Thomas Shroubsell, infans.

The 31th of Januarie was buried William Chillenden, housholder.

The 2^d of feb was buried Sarles Humfray the son of Andrew Humfray, child.

The 3^d of feb was buried Alice Spencer the Daught^r of Willm Spencer, child.

The 19th of feb was buried a poore man, a strang^r.

The 2^d of March was bur. Willm Bush, household^r.

The 20th of March was buried Elizabeth Carter, a poore woman.

The 22th of March was buried Tomsyn Raynolds the Daught^r of Georg Raynolds.

1598. Here entreth the yere of our L. 1598.

The 3^d of Aprill was buried Wm Badkyn the son of Rychard Badkyn, child.

The 18th of Aprill was buried Alice Lye, wid.

The 26th of Septĕb^r was buried Thomas Tompson the son of Thomas Tompson.

The 29th of Septĕber was buried Mathie Adie the sonne of Mathie Adie, infans.

The 4th of Octob^r was buried Ann Benkyn, wid.

WILLIAM PLACE.
RICHARD RUCK.
THOMAS HENDMAN. ⊕

Page 81.

The 16th of Nouĕmb was buried Joan Clyfford, wid.

The 17th of Decĕb was buried Elizabeth Shroubsoll the wyfe of Richard Shroubsoll.

The 5th of ffebruar was buried John Clagate, housh^r.

The 19th of feb was buried Ann Preble the Daught^r of John Preble, infant.

The 18th of March was buried Margeret Jacob Daught^r of Cirriack Jacob, Infant.

1599. Here entrethe the yere of our L. 1599.

The second of Aprill was buried John Tennaker the son of Edward Tennaker, Infant.

The 4th of April was buried Alyce Jeffrye, wid.

The 24th of Aprill was buried John Davyson, stranger.

The 22th of May was buried Roger Austen.

The 4th of June was buried Richard Badkyn, housh^r.

The 21th of June was buried Laurence Brooke, housh^r.

The xvjth of Julye was buried Elizabeth Shroubsoll, Daugh^r of Edw: Shroubsoll.

The 19th of Julie was buried Margaret Lewes, Daught^r of James Lewes, infans.

The 6ᵗʰ of August was buried Edward Tennaker son of John Tennaker, houshold͏ʳ.

The first of Septeƀ was buried a poore man whose name we know not.

The 11ᵗʰ of October was A strang child.

The 12ᵗʰ of Octoƀ was buried Georg Jnes (?) a stranger.

The 12ᵗʰ of Nouꝱmbʳ was buried John Shroubsell son of Edward Shroubsell, child.

The 13ᵗʰ of Nouꝱber was buried Thomas Lawe the son of Ralf Law, child.

The 30ᵗʰ of Decꝱber was burᵈ Jane Shroubsoll the Daughtʳ of Roƀt Shroubsoll.

The 3ᵈ of Januar. was buried Joan Howesse, wid.

The 15ᵗʰ of Januar. was buried Georg Mills, Juuenis.

The 27ᵗʰ of Januar. was buried Joan Edwards the wife of John Edwards.

The viᵗʰ of Feƀ was buried Thomas Pysing son of . . . Pysing, Juuenis.

The 18ᵗʰ of feƀ was burᵈ William Pope son of Mathew Pope.

The 27ᵗʰ of feƀ was burᵈ Georg Shefford, houshold͏ʳ.

Here entreth 1600.   1600.

The fourth of May was buried Christopher Hendman Juuenis.

The 18ᵗʰ Day was buried Annie Keeler, Wid.

The 6ᵗʰ of June was buried Arthure Place son of John Place, Jun.

The 12ᵗʰ of June was buried Sixborowe Collens wyfe of Edward Collens.

Page 82.

The 10ᵗʰ of Septꝱber was buried Dorothie Pettyt, Daughtʳ of Henrie Pettyt, gent.

The 23ᵗʰ of Septꝱber was buried Margerie Shroubsell the wife of John Shroubsell, sen.

The xiij of Octoƀ was buried Abram Spencer son of John Spencer.

The 23ᵗʰ of Octoƀ was burᵈ Joan Travesse the wife of Edw: Travesse.

The xviij of Decꝱber was buried Robert Norman, housholder.

The ixᵗʰ of Octoƀ buried Joan Hammon, an old maide.

Certified at Easter 160i.

Here entreth the yere of our Lord 160i.   160i.

The xᵗʰ of April was buried John ffulkham, puer.

The 27ᵗʰ of May was buried Thomsin Edwards the wife of John Edwards.

The 2ᵈ of June was buried William Enfield, houshold͏ʳ.

The 11ᵗʰ of June was buried Ann Tayler daughter of Daniell Tayler, child.

The 15ᵗʰ of July was buried Joan Watson daughtʳ of Hammon Watson, child.

The 4ᵗʰ of Septꝱbʳ was buried Rychard Carter, Juuenis.

The third of October buried a poore soldier.
The 11th of October was buried William Cornish, household^r.
The 17th of Octob buried a poore soldier whose name we know not.
The 15th of Nouëb^r was buried Tho: Tompson, puer.
The 21th of Nouëber was buried Edward Collens son of Edward
·· Collens, infans.
The 24th of Nouëber was buried . . . Besant . . . of Georg Besant,
infans.
The first of feb was buried Sara Potter the wife of Thomas Potter.
The same day was buried Ann Place the daughter of John Place,
sen., infans.
The 16th of feb was buried Joan Adie, Daughter of Mathie Adie,
infans.
The 17th of ffeb was buried Edward Brodstreet son of John Brod-
street, infans.
The xth of March was buried Margaret Smith, wid., Annosa mulier.

thus far certified.

Here entreth the yere of our L. 1602.

The 9th of May was buried Martyn Hurl.
The 13 of May buried Marie Adie daughter of Mathie Adie, infans.
The 15th of June buried Stephan Norman son of Edward Norman.
The 11th of June buried Edward Dine, houshold^r.
The 7th of Julye buried Rabish Besant the wyfe of Georg Besant.
The 10th of Julye bur. Robt: Clyfford, household^r.

Page 83.

The 22^d of August bur^d Elizabeth Maxsted daught^r of John Maxsted
Ju, infans.
The 29th of August bur^d Nicholas Tadd, householder.
The 15th of Octob^r bur^d Elizabeth Marshall wife of Matthew Marshall.
The 22th of Octob^r bur^d John Vigars, senex.
The 24th of Octob^r bur^d Thomas Downe.
The 9th of Decemb^r bur^d William Collens son of Edmund Collens,
infans.
The 2^d of Januarie bur. Alyce Howesse Daughter of Richard
Howesse, child.
The 31th of Januarie bur^d Parnell Balden the wyfe of John Balden.
The 26th of ffeb bur^d Richard Wollet, Juuenis.
The 20th of March bur^d Alice Travesse daughter of Edward Travesse.
The 22th of March bur^d John Kyng, adolescens.

Here entreth the yere of our L. 1603.

The 27th of March bur^d Ann Goose daughter of Tho: Goose, child.
The 28th of March bur^d Edward Besant son of Georg Besant, puer.
The 28th of Aprill bur^d Peter Trewell, a stranger who died in the
high way.
The first of May buried Margaret Tennaker, child.

Thus far certified the 6th of May 1603.

The 20th of May buried Thomas Norman, housholder.
The 21th of May bur^d Dorothy Dilet, Virgo.
The 27th of May bur^d Stephan Clement, housholder.
The 29th of June bur^d Arthure Loue son of Georg Loue,infans.
The 6th of Julye bur^d Elizabeth Woodwall, virgo.
The 14th of July bur^d Marie Wiget, virgo.
The 25th of July bur^d Edward Dunkyn, household^r.
The 5th of August bur^d Jean a stranger who died traveyling throgh our pish.
The 13th of Octob bur^d Marie Adams, Virgo.
The same day bur^d Thomas Norcote, infans.
The 27th of Octob bur^d James Web, a stranger.
The 2^d of Noueb bur^d Richard Penn.
The 11th of Noueb bur^d a poore travayling woman whose name we know not.
The 13th of Noueb bur^d John Carter, houshold^r.
The same day bur^d Joan Pope wife of Tho: Pope, Ju.
The 28th of Noueb buried William Rye, infans.
The 15th of Deceb bur^d Sara Huxborow, Virgo.
The 21th of Deceber bur. Alice Carter wife of Jo: Carter.
The 26th of Januar. bur^d Margaret fryth, puella.
The 16th of ffeb bur^d Grace Brockwell, infans.
The 19th of ffeb bur^d Alice Spencer, infans.
The 19th of March bur^d Richard Brockwell, houshold^r.

Here entreth the yere of Or Lord 1604.   1604.

The 31 of March bur^d Mathie Adie, housholder.
The 6th of Aprill bur^d Phebe Hussye, puella.
The 9th of Aprill bur. Alice Woodwall, infans.
The 10th of Aprill bur. Tomsyn Collens, infans.
The 16th of Aprill bur. Grace Brockwell.
The 9th of June bur^d Marie Walsall, Daught^r of Walsall.
The 26 of June bur. Mathew Carter.
The 22 of July bur^d John Hurst son of John Hurst.
The 23th of August bur. Edmund Hunt.

Page 84.

The 20th of August buried Susan Pantry daught^r of Rose Pantry.
The 26th of Octob^r buried Stephan Juce, houshold^r.
The 9th of Decemb bur^d Jsaac Baker, puer.
The 10th of March bur^d Austen King, houshold^r.
The 23th of March bur^d Ann Norman, wid.

thus far certified.

Here entreth the year of our L. 1605.   1605.   1605.

The viijth of Aprill bur^d Ann Juce, wid.
The 11th of Aprill bur^d Margaret Ruck, infans.
The 24th of Aprill bur^d Grace Norcote, Daughter of Thomas Norcote, Ju., infans.

The 30th of Aprill bur^d John Tennaker & Ann his wife.
The 9th of May bur^d Ann Spencer, infans Daughter of Wiłłm Spencer.
The 25th of May bur^d Wiłłm Maxted son of John Maxted.
The 5th of June buried Marie Smithson Daughter of John Smithson, puella.
The 6th of July buried Richard Marshall son of Mathew Marshall, Adolescens.
The 16th of Septeb^r buried Elizabeth Woodwall wife of Mathew Woodwall.
The 2^d of Octob^r buried John Bayley, houshold^r.
The 31th of Octob^r buried . . . Tritton, wid.
The 27th of Deceb^r buried Wiłłm Okenfold, houshold^r.
The 30th of Deceb^r buried Peter Edwards, Adolescens.
The first of ffeb buried Marie Elsten the wife of Thomas Elsten.
The 20th of ffeb buried Hamon Downe son of wid. Downe, puer.
The 21th of ffeb buried Sara Hobbs wife of Tho : Hobbs.
The 6th of March bur^d . . . Knot, Daughter Stephan Knot, infans.
The 8th of March bur^d John Hussye, houshold^r.

Here entreth the yere of our L. God 1606. 1606.

The 16th of May buryed Alice Thomas Daugh. of John Thomas.
The 5th of Julye bur^d Tomsyu Carter, maidserv.
The 27th of July buried Thomas Maxsted sone of John Maxsted.
The 25th of Sept. buried Will ffroud son of Joseph ffroud.
The 26 of Oct. bur^d Obedience Clyfford Daught. of Tho Clyfford.
The 30th of Oct. bur. Marie Kennard wyfe of John Kennard.
The 16th of Deceb^r bur^d John Bradford.
The 18th of ffeb bur^d Tho : Hittell, a poore man.

1607. 1607. 1607.

The 15th of June buryed Richard Day son of John Day, infãt.
The 28th of June bur^d John Maxsted, houshold^r.
The 8th of July bur^d Tomsyu Hills Daught. of Michaell Hills, infant.
The 10th of July bur^d Michal Norrise son of Michaell Norrise, infant.
The 20th of July bur^d Mark Tayler son of Daniell Tayler, infant.
The 7th of August bur^d Edward Travesse son of Edward Travesse, infant.
The 25th of Octob bur^d Elizabeth Hills, Daughter of Michaell Hills, infant.
The 2^d of Noueb^r bur^d Ann Shroubsoll daughter of Thomas Shroubsoll.
The 13 of Noueb^r buryed Henrie Petite, Esquier.
The 22th of Noueb^r bur^d Elizab : Spencer wyfe of Adam Spencer.
The 12th of Deceb^r bur^d John Keñard, houshold^r.
The 18th of Jan. bur^d William Juce son of John Juce, Juuenis.
The 24th of Jan. bur^d Georg Pen son of . . . Pen, infans.
The 29th of Jan. buried Tho : Elsten, houshold^r.

Page 85.

The first of ffeb bur. Julian Bensted, wid.
The 16ᵗʰ of feb burᵈ Cornelius Caco, adolescens.
The 25ᵗʰ of feb bur. Margaret Pope wyfe of Tho : Pope.

Here entreth the yere of our L. 1608 1608.

thus far certified.

The 6ᵗʰ of Aprill burᵈ . . . Wood, widow.
The 2ᵈ of July burᵈ Elizabeth fryar, virgo.
The 4ᵗʰ of July bur. Marie Smithson virgo.
The 9ᵗʰ of July bur. Georg Ruck, infans.
The 16ᵗʰ of July bur. Joan Downe wyfe of Christopher Downe.
The 19ᵗʰ of July bur. Henry day, puer.
The 3ᵈ of August bur. A stranger, a woman.
The 14ᵗʰ of August bur. Marie Nox wyfe of John Nox.
The 15ᵗʰ of August bur. Tho: Horsley, senex.
The 22ᵗʰ of Octobʳ bur. Elizabeth Pope, infans.
The 11ᵗʰ of Novēbʳ bur. Alice Wood, infans.
The 5ᵗʰ of Decēbʳ bur. Henrie Davis, Juvenis.
The 31ᵗʰ of Deēbʳ bur. Tho : Hendman, Juvenis.
The 5ᵗʰ of ffeb bur. a stranger named chapman.
The 26ᵗʰ of feb. bur. Avis Smith, virgo.
The 8ᵗʰ of March bur. Catharine Roger, infans.
The same Day bur. Dennis & Elizabeth burd, infantes.
The 12ᵗʰ of March bur. John Burd.

thus far certifyed.

Here entreth 1609. 1609.

The 7ᵗʰ of May buried Richard Hills son of Michaell Hills, infans.
The 25ᵗʰ of May bur. Joan Shroubsoll daughter of . . . Shroubsoll, infans.
The 5ᵗʰ of June bur. Ralf Chillenden, housholdʳ.
The 6ᵗʰ of June bur. Thomas Pope theldʳ, housholdʳ.
The 27ᵗʰ of June bur. fflorence Nox daughter of John Nox, infans.
The 29ᵗʰ of June buryed William Shroubsell, housholdʳ.
The 30ᵗʰ of June bur. a poore wandring boy called Griffyn.
The 6ᵗʰ of July bur. Richard Shroubsoll son of Thomas Shroubsoll, puer.
The 13ᵗʰ of July buried wid. Browne.
The 3ᵈ of Septembʳ bur. Robt Nicholas.
The 10ᵗʰ of Septēbʳ bur. Amye Woodwall, wid.
The same day bur. Thomsyn Woodwall, puella.
The 11ᵗʰ of Septembʳ buried Henrie Nicholas son of Robt Nicholas, puer.
The 14ᵗʰ of Septembʳ bur. A poore Jrishmā.
The 16ᵗʰ day of Septeb buryed Margerie Packnam, Daughter of Roger Packnam, puella.

The 19th of Septēbr bur. Richard Nicholas son of Robert Nicholas.
The 12th of Septēbr bur. Amie Woodwall daughter of Mathy Wood-
wall, infans.
The 22th of Septemb buried Jonas Parks son of Dorcas Parkes, puer.
The same Day bur. Catharine Packnam daughtr of Roger Packnam.

Page 86.

The 26th of Septembr burd a poore Irish child.
The 27th of Septembr burd John Woodwall son of Mathy Woodwall,
infans.
The 20th of Octob bur. Dorcas Parks, wid.
The 25th of Octob buryed Moses Shroubsoll the son of Christopher
Shroubsoll, infans.
The 23th of Octob buryed Raynold Abram, housholdr.
The 24th of Octob was buryed . . .
The 29th of Octob burd Christopher Downes, housholdr.
The 18th of Nouemb burd Thomas Norcote the elder.
The 26th of Novemb bur. Elizabeth Knott, wid.
The 20th of Decemb buryed . . . the wyfe of John Juce.
The 24th of Decemb bur. Mizdrach Giles, Juuenis.
The 18th of Januarie buried John Hether, housholdr.
The 29th of Januar. buryed Henrie Pay.
The 30th of Januarie bur. Edward Brodstreete, housholdr.
The 12th of ffeb bur. Alice the wyfe of Nicholas Juce.
The 12th of March burd Elizabeth Bensted daughter of John Bensted,
infans.
The 19th of March bur. William Bensted son of John Bensted, infans.

thus far certifyed.

Here entreth the yere or L. 1610. 1610. 1610.

The 26th of March burd Sara Bensted daughter of John Bensted,
infans.
The 2d of Aprill burd Marke White son of . . . White, infans.
The 7th of Aprill bur. Edward Allen, adolescens.
The 13th of Aprill burd John Hare, senex.
The 15th of Aprill burd Elizabeth Pope wyfe of Nicholas Pope.
The 19th of Aprill burd Ralf Pantry, householdr.
The 31th of August burd Joan Hubbert, infans.
The 9th of Septeb burd Edward Kennytt, Juuenis.
The first of Octob burd . . . March.
The 10th of Noueb burd Margerie Adie, infans.
The 15th of Noueb buryed Edward Travesse, housholdr.
The 17th of Nouemb burd Elizabeth Hix, infans.
The 21 of Noveb burd Ann Travesse, wid.
The 30th of Noueb burd Jsraell Blanket, infans.
The 14th of Deceb bur. Susan Tayler, uxor.
The 24th of Deceb buryed Alexandr Downe, senex.
The 30th of Deceb bur. Elizabeth Richardson, infans.
The 20 of Jan. burd Zacharie Essex, wid.

The 28th of Januarie bur. Joan Pantry, infans.
The first of feb buryed John Balden, houshold^r.

Page 87.

The 7th of feb buryed Susan Tayler, infans.
The 23 of feb bur^d Elizabeth Douglasse, infans.

Thus far certified.

Here entreth the yere of o^r L. 1611.

The 4th of Aprill buryed Thomas Golson, infans.
The 16th of May buryed Thomas King, infans.
The 11th of June buryed Thomas Mount, Juvenis.
The xth of Octob buryed Humfry Clerk, houshold^r.
The 21th of Octob buryed Phebe Spencer, infans.
The xiiijth of Novemb bur. Water Wingfeild, houshold^r.
The xviijth of Novemb buryed Marke Juce, houshold^r.
The vjth of Decemb buryed Alice Chappell, wid.
The xjth of Decemb buryed Robert Sharp.
The xvjth of Januarie buryed Joan Shroubsoll.
The 19th of Januarie buryed John Paine, infans.
The xxvth of Januar. buryed Alice Gray, puella.
The xvijth of feb buryed John Spencer, houshold^r.
The xxvjth of feb buryed Abigaile Golson, infans.
The first of March buryed Alice Keler, uxor.
The 8th of March buried Thomas Elnar, infans.
The xxijth of March bur. John Edwards, Juvenis.

Certified thus far.

Here entreth 1612. 1612.

The 27th of March buryed Ann Elnar, infans.
The 14th of Aprill buryed William Millen, Adolescens.
The 24th of Aprill buryed Barbara Shroubsell, wid.
The xth of May buryed Michael Nash, puer.
The same day buryed Ann Evens, infans.
The 3^d of June buried Edward Tilson, houshold^r.
The 7th of June buryed Mathew Woodwall.
The 3^d of July bur. Richard Howesse, houshold^r.
The 9th of Septeb bur^d Thomas, a stranger.
The 15th of Septeb bur. Joyce Place, puella.
The 22th of Septemb^r bur. Walther Bigge.
The 20th of Octob bur. Robert Layton, infans.
The 16th of Novēb^r bur^d Alice Bensted, infans.
The 25th of Decemb^r bur^d Joan Pollard, wid.
The 29th of Decemb^r bur. Tomsyn Vigars, wid.
The 30th of Decēb^r bur. Alice Hursley, widow.
The 3^d of ffeb bur. John Golson, houshold^r.
The 4th of March bur. Jean Longley, puella.
The 2ith of March bur. ffrances Pettite, Adolesens.

Thus far certified.

Here entreth 1613   1613.

The 25th of March bur. Ann Robinson, uxor.
The same Day bur. James Lewes, houshold^r.
The 28th of March bur. Joan Shroubsoll.
The 9th of Aprill bur. Cir. Jacob, houshold^r.
The 12th of Aprill bur. Margaret Ping, uxor.
The 3th July buried Alice ffryte daughter of Thomas ffryte, Jnfans.
The 30th of July bury^d Mary daught^r of ye said Tho. ffryte, Jnfans.
The 31th of July bur^d George Pynge, houshold^r.

Page 88.

The 16 of August buried Jasabe Cork.
The 7th of September bur. Mary Pettet Daughter of Henry Pettet, esquier.
The 11th of Sept. bur^d a Straunger.
The 10th of Oct. Bur^d Elizabeth Meare wif of Leonard Meare.
The 20th of Octob bur : Myles Golson sonne of Edward Golsonne.
The 1th of Novemb bur : Thomas Shrubsole son of Thomas Shrubsole.
The 4th of Nouemb^r bur : Catharine Hussey, widd.
The 30th of January bur. Mathew Mshall sonne of Mathew Marshall.
The 16th of March bur. Elizabeth Golson wyf of Edward Golsonne.
The 21th of March bur : Willm Edwards sonne of John Edwards.

Certified thus far.

1614.   Here entreth 1614.

The 25th of March bur^d John Edwards, Clarke of the parrishe.
The same Day bur^d John Hussy, Jun.
The 27th of March buryed Edward Songer an Aged man.
The 6th of Apprill bur^d Elizabeth Miller wyf of Lawrance Miller.
The 12th of May buried Symon Packnam the sonne of Nicholas Packnam.
The 22th of May bur^d Augustie Morto, senex.
The 13th daye of June buryed Henrie Renouls, Senex.
The 19th daie of June buried Captaine Edward Osborne who was Slaine.
The 11th of July buried Alice Edwards, Widdowe.
The 14th of July buried John Kinge, Senex, Bachalarius.
The 20th daie of September buried Jsabell Poope wif of Mathew Poope.
The 20th day of December buried Ann Meare, Daughter of Leonard Meare.
The 6th daie of January buried Barbara the wiffe of John Tayler.
The 17th daie of January wer buried to male & Crism, Twynes, the sonnes of Jefery Mollenger.
The 3th day of ffebruary buried mother Newman, widowe.
The 21th of ffebruarie buried Rebeca Lewies, Daughter of Jsacke Lewies.
The 26th of ffebr. buried Benett the wif of Andrew Pett.

The 6ᵗʰ of March was buried Marie Peirce, Daughter of James Peirce. The same Daie was buried harice borne at Borden.

Page 89.

The 21ᵗʰ daie of March buried Stephen Grimesell, senex paterfamilias. Thus far certified.

Heare entereth 1615.

The 27ᵗʰ of March buried Alice ffittell wife of John ffittell.
The 16ᵗʰ daie of Aprill buried Sara Pope daughter of Mathew Pope, infans.
The first of Maie buried Thomas Chillenden son of Tho. Chillenden.
The 11ᵗʰ Daie of May buried Wᵐ Tyttell of ffishpen.
The 25ᵗʰ of Julie buried Adam & Wᵐ Spenser the sons of Richard Spenser, Esq., Jnfantes.
The 12ᵗʰ Daie of August buried Thomas Goose, houshoulder.
The 13ᵗʰ Daie of the same burᵈ ffrances Daughter of Thomas Norcott.
The 20ᵗʰ Daie of the same buried Johane Renouls, widow.
The 3ᵗʰ Daye of September buried Elizabeth Daughter of Rich: Howls.
The 4ᵗʰ of the same burᵈ Margery King, widowe.
The 10ᵗʰ of the same buried Edward son of Thomas Webb, Ju.
The 13ᵗʰ of the same buried Richard son of Thomas ffearne.
The 15ᵗʰ Day of the same buried mothʳ Envell, widowe.
The 18ᵗʰ Daie of the same buried Mʳ William Wood, houshoulder.
The same daie buried X͡pofer the sonne of William Gill.
The 26ᵗʰ of the same buriede Elizabeth wife of X͡pofer Kinge.
The same Daie buried Willᵐ sonne of the said X͡pofer King, Jnfa.
The 29ᵗʰ of the same burᵈ Robert Shrubsole, houshoulder.
The 4ᵗʰ of October buried mother Tim, widowe.
The 7ᵗʰ of the same burᵈ William Chillenden son of John Chillenden.

Page 90.

The 14ᵗʰ Daie of the same buried Alice Gouldesmith, Daughter of Wiłłm Gouldesmith.
The 16ᵗʰ Daie of the same burᵈ Wiłłm Grimesell son of Steph. Grimesell, Bacalarius.
The 18ᵗʰ Daie of the same buried Roƀt Newman son of Andrew Newman, infans.
The 23ᵗʰ of the same buried a male Childe son of Leonard Meare, unchristened.
The first of Novemƀ bur. Joane Dau. of James Boykett.
The 15ᵗʰ of the same buried Richard Williams, houshoulder.
The last of yᵉ same buried Ann wiffe of the said James Boykett.
The 17ᵗʰ Daie of December buried Elizabeth, Daughter of Henry Aritare.
The 25ᵗʰ Daie of the same buried Misack Lawe, Singleman.
The jᵗʰ Daie of Januarie buried William Palmer & Jane his wife.
The same Daie buried Anthony Goulson son of John Goulson.

The 2ᵗʰ Daie of the same burᵈ Wᵐ & Susan Palmeʳ the childrẽ of the said Wᵐ Palmʳ.

The 12ᵗʰ Daie of the same buried Marie, Daughter of Michaell Porter, infans.

The 13ᵗʰ Daie of the same burᵈ Thomas Crippen of the pishe of Ospreng.

The 14ᵗʰ Daie of the same burᵈ Wiłłm Traves, son of Ed. Traves.

The 27ᵗʰ of the same buried Ann Dilett wife of Symon Dylett.

The 19ᵗʰ of the same buried Mathew Marshall, Senex Paterfamilias.

The 12ᵗʰ of March burᵈ Mothʳ Pollard, widdowe.

The 14ᵗʰ of the same burᵈ John Day, housholder.

The 15ᵗʰᵉ of the same burᵈ Thomas Shubsoll, housholder.

The 18ᵗʰ of the same burᵈ An Daughtʳ of William Hamon.

The 22ᵗʰ of the same buried Ann Howesse, widdowe.

The 25ᵗʰᵉ of the same burᵈ a man cheild the son of Mathew Poope not baptized.

Thus far Directlie set downe.

Page 91.

Here entreth the yeare of oʳ Lord god 1616.

The 28 Daie of March buried Willᵐ sonne of Mathewe Boyse.

The 12ᵗʰ daie of Apprill buried Mary daughter of Xpofer Shrubsole of Scokers hill.

The same day burᵈ Adam son of John Place, senior.

The 13ᵗʰ of the same buried Mary daug. of the said John Place.

The 20ᵗʰ day of the same buried John Thomas, housholder.

The 25ᵗʰ of the same buried Ralph Lawe, housholder.

The 27ᵗʰ of the same buried Larence Juice, housholder.

The 15ᵗʰ daie of June buried Ellen Maxted the wiffe of Richard Maxted.

The last of June was buried a male crisamer child the son of Richard Senr :

The 9ᵗʰ of July was buried Willᵐ Wyse, houshoulder.

The 10 of the same was buried Katerine the daughter of Mary Dylett wif of Henry Dylett.

The 21ᵗʰ day of the same buried Xpian the wif of John Hicke.

The same daie buried Ursela Tods, widowe.

The 7ᵗʰ daie of August buried William the sone of Thomas ffrith.

The 23ᵗʰ of the same buried ffrance Pettet a younge maiden the Daughter of Henry Pettet, Esquier.

The 30ᵗʰ of the same buried Marian Hilles, Senex vidua.

The 15ᵗʰ daye of September buried Thomas Downe the sonne of Edward Downe of Sellinge.

The 8ᵗʰ daie of October buried Dame Ann Ladie Hawkyns the wiffe of Sir Thomas Hawkyns, Knight.

The 16ᵗʰ daie of the same buried Georg, a poore vagrant boye.

The 17ᵗʰ of the same buried a female Chrisamer the daughter of Jervis Whatlowe.

The 23ᵗʰ daie of the same buried Ann the wif of the said Jervis Whatlow.

The 29ᵗʰ daie of the same buried Margaret the wif of John Shrubsole.

The 30ᵗʰ daie of the same buried mother Goade.

The 17ᵗʰ of November buried Margret Hobbs the wiffe of Thomas Hobbs.

Page 92.

The 24ᵗʰ of November was buried Edward Shrubsole son of John Shrubsole, senʳ.

The same Daie buried Richarden Shrubsole, an oulde widowe.

The 6ᵗʰ daie of January buried Susan the wiffe of Abraham Wood.

The 26ᵗʰ of Januarie buried Elizabeth the daughter of Thomas Keeler.

The 30ᵗʰ of January buried Edward son of William Shrubsole, senʳ, deceased.

The 13ᵗʰ daye of ffebruarie buried Benet the wif of Wiłłm Tayler & a female Child not christned.

The xxviiij daye of ffebruarie buried John Tayler, widoer.

The 11ᵗʰ of March buried Amie Mempas wiffe of Thomas Mempas some tyme dwelling about the Cittie of Canterbury.

Here entreth the yeare of our Lord 1617.

The 15ᵗʰ daye of Aprill buried Dorothie the Daughter of John Goulson.

The 23ᵗʰ of Aprill was buried Sir Thomas Hawkyns, Knight.

The 11ᵗʰ of May buried John the sonne of John Dane of Tenham.

The 12ᵗʰ of May buried Marie Juyce the daghter of Larence Juyce.

The 28ᵗʰ day of May buried Mary the daughter of William Dane.

The 30ᵗʰ of May buried Mathew the sone of Daniell Marshall, Jnfans.

The 13ᵗʰ Daye of July was buried Wiłłm Ore late of Challocke.

The 14ᵗʰ day of the same bured Anne Whitall daughter of William Whitall, an outdweller.

The 3ᵗʰ of August buried Stephen the sonne of Stephen Pim, Infans.

The 16ᵗʰ daye of September buried Stephan Witherley son of Edmund Witherley, late of Challocke, deceased.

The 6ᵗʰ of October buried Mary the daughter of Mathew Boyse.

The 5ᵗʰ of November buried Margaret the wif of Richard Bensted thelder.

The 7ᵗʰ of the same buried Catharine the wif of John Kinge.

The 8ᵗʰ of the same buryed John the sonne of Gidion Tayller.

The 17ᵗʰ of the same burid Thomas Strachy, seruant to Captaine Tompsonne.

The 20ᵗʰ of the same buried Elizabeth Edward, singlewoman.

The 23ᵗʰ of the same buried Thomas Carpenter, singleman.

Page 93.

The 18 of December buried a Crysane the son of Edward Shrubsole of Boughton street.

The 11th of January buried John the sonne of Wm Pickeforks borne of a travaling woman both of Charinge, infans.

The 19th day of January buried Margaret the wife of Jervice Bradenex.

The 21th of the same buried Mary the daughter of Wm Shrubsole, Carp infã.

The 12th of ffebruary buried Thomas Keeler, houshoulder.

The 6th day of March buried A ffemale Chrisamer the daught. of Thomas Pordage.

The 19 daye of March buried Godly Skreimebey, widowe.

Here entreth the yeare of or Lord 1618.

The first day of Aprill buried Thomasen the widow of Ralph Lawe.

The 15th of Aprill buried . . . Maneringe a poore widowe.

The 25th day of Aprill buried Thomas Maxted sonne of Robt. Maxted of Crooche.

The 11th daye of Maye buried Stephan Keeler, houshoulder.

The 24th day of May buried Richard Robinsonne, Senex.

The 21t day of July buried Dorothie the daughter of Thomas Spencer.

The 10th day of Sept. buried . . . Johnson, widowe.

The 15th daye of the same burd Anne the wife of Michaell Hills.

The 20th day of Septembr buried Katharine the then wife of John Hendman.

The 27th day of September buried Sara Price the daughter of Mathew Price, Jnfans.

The 4th day of October buried Elizabeth Mountt daught. of John Movnt, Jnfans.

The 15th of Novembr burd Richard the sonne of Richard Lattenton, Jnfans.

The 23th of Novembr burd Wm the son of Willm Spenser.

The 29th of Novembr burd a male Chrism the sonne of Robert Spenser.

The last of December burd Thomas Wynckfild, an outdweller.

The 16th of January buried Katharine the wife of William Mears.

The last day of January burd James Richard & John the sonnes of Jsaack Lewis, Jnfantes.

The 2jth of ffebruary burd Edward Chillenden, an outdweller.

Año Dom. 1619.

The 10th of Aprill buried John Wise the sonne of Wm Wise.

Page 94.

The 7th day of June buried Dorothie Price the daughter of Mathew Price.

The 10th day of June buried Edward Collens, houshoulder.

H

The 11th day of June buried Robert Adams the sonne of John Adams, Jnfans.

The 16th day of June bur^d Robert Pordage, Batcheler.

The 18th Day of June bur^d Sibell Ledgegood, Daughter of Giles Ledgegood, infans.

The 22th day of June bur^d Anne the daughter of Henry Bayley.

The 4th of July buried Nicholas the sonne of Anne Woodwall, base-borne.

The 15th of July buried Grace Wood, Widdowe.

The 21th day of July buried Richard Shrubsole, senex.

The 23th day of July buried Susan Andrewe.

The 11th of August buried Joane Kinge the daughter of Xp̄ofer Kinge.

The 13th of August buried the widowe Bradford.

The 29th of August buried Abrahã Bradford.

The 2th day of October buried Dorothie Carpenter, Singlewoman.

The 4th day of October bur^d a Male Child the son of Robert Spenser not Christned.

The 5th of October buried Margaret Pemble, a poore widowe.

The 16th day of October bur^d Joane Maxted the wife of Robert Maxted of Beechwood.

The 20th of October buried John Shrubsole son of John Shrubsole, Jũior.

The 27th day of October bur^d Elizabe the daughter of Johane Wild, baseborne.

The 30th day of October buried Thomas ffowler.

The 2th day of Nouember buried John Place, sen.

The 8th day of November bur^d Gillian Downe of the pishe of Sellinge, Widdowe.

The 10th of Nouember bur^d Wm Carr the son of Augusten Carr, Jnfans.

The 11 of November bur^d Thomas Trepedye houshoulder.

The 16th day of November buried Marie Spencer the daughter of Richard Spencer, virg.

The 5th day of Decemb^r buried Edward Downe of Sellinge.

The 13th of Decemb^r buried Mary Place, widowe.

The same daye bur^d Elizabeth Shrubsole, daughter of John Shrubsole, Junior, Jnfans.

The 4th of January buryed Rob̄t Maxted of Crooche.

The 17th of January bur^d Mary daught. of Sarum Baseden.

The 14th Day of ffebruarie buried Andrew Pett.

Here entreth the yeare of o^r Lord 1620.

The 29th day of March buried Katharen the wif of Nicholas Shrub-sole.

The 30th day of Aprill buried Martha Shrubsole the daughter of Nicholas Shrubsole aforesaid.

The 25th day of May burd^d Edward the sonne of Ezeckiell Maxted, Jnfans.

The 29th day of May buried Wm Hawe ats Halle.

The 30th of May buried Wm Connaway the sonne of William Connaway.

The 6th of June a male child son of John Brodestreet, not baptized, was buried.

The same day buried James Reade, singleman.

Page 95.

The 11 of June buried Elizbath Shrubsole the daughter of Edward Shrubsole of Boughton street.

The 21th day of June buried Richard Maxted, senex.

The 28th day of July bur^d Thomsen Hicks daught. of John Hicks.

The 5th day of August bur^d Elizabet Ping.

The same day buried Abraham Bensted sonne of Richard Bensted, Junr.

The 14th day of August Agnes Downe, widowe.

The 10th day of September buried Richard Pordage sonne of Thomas Pordage, Juvenis, was buried.

The 14th day of Sept. buried Thomas Clinton.

The 20th day of Octob. bur^d John Binge sonne of William Binge, Infans.

The 29th day of October bur^d Thomas Oore.

The 14th day of Nouemb^r buried Mary Juice, vid.

The 18th day of Nouemb. bur^d Jobane Auinge, vid.

The 21th day of Novemb^r Symon Dylett, senex.

The first day of Decemb^r bur^d Johane Pordage daughter of Thomas Pordage.

The 11th day of December a male child the sonne of Robert Spencer not baptized.

The 4th day of January was bur^d Thomas Henman, h'ou.

The 9th day of January bur^d a male Chield the sonne of William Place, Juñ, not baptized.

The 4th day of ffebruary was buried Alice Pordage daughter of Thomas Pordage, viř.

The 5th day of ffebruary was buried Elizabeth Wood, singlewoman.

The 4th day of March bur^d Richard Greenstret the sonne of a vagarant woman.

The 15th day of March bur^d widow ffoules.

Here entreth the yeare of o^r Lord 162i.

The 15th day of May bur^d John Brodstreete, housh.

The 23 of August bur^d William Jacob, housholder.

The 24th of August bur^d Phebe the wife of William Ashton.

The 29th of August bur^d Sara the daught^r of Richard Mountt, an outdweller.

The 26th day of Septemb^r Thomas Sommers the sonne of Henry Soñers of ffeuersham was buried.

The 16th day of Octob[r] was bur[d] Alice Shrubsole, wid.

The same day was bur[d] William Spenser the sonne of Robert Spenser.

The 8th day of Novemb[r] bur[d] ffrance Roper the daughter of Henry Roper, gent.

The 9th day of Novemb[r] bur[d] a male Child the sonne of Michaell Porter, not baptized.

The 19th day Novemb[r] bur[d] Jobane Smithe.

The second day of Decemb[r] bur[d] Sara Brodstreet, the Daughter of John Brodstreet, posthumar.

The 30th day of Decemb[r] buried Mathew Leget, senex.

The 3th day of January buried William Petett sonne of William Pettet, gent. Jnfans.

The 4th day of January bur[d] Catheren ffry, singlewomã.

The 7th day of Januarie bur[d] Thomas Pope, houshold.

The 24th day of January Elenor the daughter of Henry Shrubsole.

The 27th day of January bur[d] Thomas Saton, senex, bacalar.

The 25th day of ffeb[r] bur[d] a male child the sonne of Richard Mount, an outdweller, not bapd.

The 11th day of March bur[d] a female child daughter of Tho. wellard, not christned.

Page 96.

Here entreth the yere of O[r] Lord 1622.   1622.

The 25th of March buried Dennis the wife of Richard Saverye.

The 19th of Aprill buryed Johan Winckfeld, wid.

The 12 of May buried John Place, houshold[r].

The 14th of May buried Joan the wife of Laurence Cornish.

The 4th of June buried Tomsyn Collens, Wid.

The 5th of June buried Laurence Cornish.

The —[th] of June buried Marie the wife of W[m] Place.

The —[th] of August bur. Elizabeth Collyer.

The 30th of August buryed Dorothie Breckwell.

The 6th of Octob[r] buried Elizabeth the wife of John Hendman.

The 24th of Octob[r] buried Elizabeth Shroubsole.

The 27th of October buried Elizabeth Hendman, infans.

The 15th of Nouemb[r] buried a vagrant man whose name we know not.

The 3[d] of Januarie buried Georg Sherlocke, infans.

The 22th of Januarie buried Laurence ffoster, Juuenis.

The 28th of Januarie buried Elizabeth the wife of Nicholas Shroubsoll.

The 31th of Jan. buried John Knott.

The first of ffeb buried Henrie Dilett.

The 15th of ffeb buried Roger Packnam.

The 16th of feb buried Joan the wife of Michaell Hills.

The 13 of March buried Susan daughter of Adam Spenc[r].

The 19th of March buryed Ann Atherne.

Here entreth the yere of o[r] Lord 1623.

The 12 of Aprill buried Nicholas Baker.

The 13 of May John the son of Henrie Shroubsoll.

The 5th of Octob[r] buried Alice Spencer, wid.

The 24th of August buried Margaret White, vxor.

The 12th of Nouember buried John Simons.

The 19th of December buried Thomas Juce.

The 20th of Januarie buried Rebacca Meere the wife of Leonard Meere.

The 16th of ffeb buried Gabriell Ruck.

The i6th of March buried Sara Rayner the wife of John Rayner.

The 16th day of Apell was buried Joan Brooke.

The 20th of March was buried Joane Kene.

Here entereth the yeare of our Lord 1624. 1624. 1624.

The 27th of Apel was buried Elizabethe Brooke the wife of John Brooke.

The 13 day of Jun was buried Ellis Clays, wido.

The 8th day of July was Buried Wilam mount Sonn of Richard Mount.

The 14 of July was buryed Danel Rider Sonne of Vallentin Rider.

The i5 of July was buryed Richard Sauerry.

The i7 of July was buryed marian Powne, the wif of Jhon Powne.

The i8 of August was buried Hue Johnson.

The 20 of August was buried Edward Juce.

The 22 of August was buried Alice Gatman Daughter of John Gatmane.

The 24 of August was buried John Down Son of John Downne.

The 30th of August was buried John Gatman.

The 15 of September was buried James Place.

The 23 of Setember was buried Elisabeth Lewes.

The 2[d] of October was Buried Hamon natson.

Page 97.

The 13 of October was buried John Ginger (?)

The i of nouember was buried John Prise, Son of mother Pris.

The 4 of nouember was buried mihel hid . . .

The 5 of nouember was buried Joan Pantry, wido.

The 7 of nouember was buried anne Shrubsol wif of nicholas Shrubsol.

The 9 of nouember was buried Elenor nokes wif of John nokes.

The 11 of nouember was buried Anne Whatman wif of James Whatman.

The 14 of nouember was buried Jllian Shrubsol daughter of nicolas Shrubsoll.

The 19 of nouember was buried thomsin downe, wido.

the 26 of nouember was buried Elizabeth Scott.

the 29 of nouember was buried the wif of wiliam . . .

the first of december was buried Patience Scot.

the 30 of december was buried a stranger.
the 7 of december was buried Susan Gooch.
the 16 of december was buried mary tayler daughter of Gedion tayler.
the 26 of december was buried Joan brodstreat, wido.
the 28 of december was buried Catherine moon wif of mihel moon.
the 30 of december was buried Arthur Whatman.
The 20 of Janeuari was buried dourthy oden daughter of . . . oden.
The 27 of Janeuari was Buried John Craft, houshoulder.
The 4 of feuari was Buried John balden.
The 7 of feuari was Buried A stranger.
The 11 of feueari was Buried ann mee^r wif of william meer.
The same day was buried Susan newmane wif of andrew newmane.
The 22 of februari was buried nicolas fayerman, boulder.
The 3 of march was buried John marsh, houshoulder.
The 6 of march was buried frances bing daughter of William bing.
The same day was buried Steeuen latende^n, Sonn of Richard Latenden.
The ix March was buried Jervis bing, houshoulder.
The 23 of March was buried Rob. tritin, Sonn of Robert tritin.

Page 98.

Heer eutreth the yeare of our lord 1625. 1625.

The 30 of march was buried thomas ouen.
The 2 of aperell burid Robert triten.
The 10 of aperel was buried isack lewes.
The 12 of apel was buried aelis (?) Cliford, widdo.
The first day of Jun was buried . . . lewes, wido.
The ninth day of Jun was buried mathew boyse.
The ninthe of July was buried Richard frith.
The 17th of July was buried Ales Spenser the wif of Roberd Spencer.
the 24th of July was buried Susan Wallend the wif of thomas wallend.
the 1th of August was buried William baldock.
the 12th of August was buried thomas Euens.
The 21th of August was buried Steeuen pecknam, houshoulder.
The 24th of September was buried William shrubsol son of william shrubsoll, Jonn^r.
the sam day was buried . . . bery sonn of mathew bery.
The 26 of september was buried mari bridgma^n.
The 2 of October was buried mari carr the wif of austen carre.
The 12 of October was buried william Cliffor^d the son of Richard Cliford.
The 15 day of october was buried Elisabeth tilson daughter of Edward tilson.
The 4th of nouember was buried Thoma^s Pordage, housholder.
The same day was buried william Carr son of John Carr.
The 9th of nouember was buried an pordage, wido.

The 10th of nouember was buried thomas perkins.
The Eleauenth of nouember wer buried Susan boyc and Joan.
The nine and twenteth day of nouember was buried Owen Shrubsol
    the son of thomas shrubsol.
The same day was buried Edward porter the son of Mihel porter.
The 15th of Janeuary was buried thomas Scott.
The 24th of Janeuary was buried James whatman.
The 4th of februay was buried henry pettit the son of william pettit,
    Gentilman.
The same day was buried mary the wif of Alexander farly.
The 21th of feuary was buried Ann Jacob.
The 3 of march was buried . . . Jefferie, a wido.
The 15 of march was buried Joan pim the wife of steuen pim.

[*End of Volume I.*]

Outside last page of cover.

    Let the dead bury the dead
    that is that they wich are
    dead in Sinn shd bury them
    that are dead for Sinn.
                John the 1 : 16.

    Remember thy Creater in
    The dayes of thy youghte
    Before the daye
    and the yeares dra night
    wher in thou shalt say
    thou hast no pleaser in thẽ.
                Eclesiastes.

    Let us not be wewry ther
    fore of well doing for in du
    season we shall repe if we
    faynte not.
           Galashians ye 6 : 9.

Mr. Place married 1593
       buried 1637   1587
                46   1637
                91

BOUGHTON-UNDER-BLEAN.

INDEX LOCORUM.

Compiled by Miss E. Hobday.

[An asterisk (*) denotes that the place occurs more than once on the page.]

Borden, 93.
Beechwood, 98.
Boughton Street, 47, 50, 97, 99.
Boughton-under-Blean (Bleene), 1*, 42, 45.
Bull, The, 82, 84.

Canterbury (Cantbury), 1, 64, 96.
Challocke, 96*.
Charinge, 97.
Crouch (Crooch, Cróoche), 46, 79, 97, 98.

Fairebrook, 81.
82, 99.
Faversham (Fevrsham, Feuersham),
Fishpen (Fyspyn), 47, 94.

Hickmans, 45.
Hodsden (Hertfordshire), 52.

Kingdowne, 64.

Northlane, 50.
Nuttree, 48.

Ospringe (Ospreng), 1, 95.

Scockete Hill (Scokers), 44, 95.
Selling (Sellinge), 20, 44, 95, 98*.
South Street (Sowth), 44, 46, 49, 50.
Stapleherst, 84.
Stile, The, 80.

Tenham, 96.
Thanet, St. Laurence, 1.
Throwley, 64.

Woodside, The, 44.

INDEX NOMINUM.

Compiled by MISS E. HOBDAY.

[An asterisk (*) denotes that the name occurs more than once on the page.]

Irregularities.—*(a) Surname and Christian name missing :* . . ., . . ., 1, 91.
(b) Surnames missing : . . ., Ann, 52 ; . . ., Christn., 54 ; . . ., Eliz., 52 ;
. . ., Hew., 77 ; . . ., Joan, 39 ; . . ., Jn., 66, 68, 76, 83 ; . . ., Margt., 2,
77 ; . . . Marion, 66 ; . . ., Nich., 71 ; . . ., Ralf, 3. 66, 67 ; . . ., Robt.,
60 ; . . ., Thos., 56, 72, 76 ; . . ., Wm., 68, 81, 101. *(c) Miscellaneous :*
R.M., 1 ; Bo . . ., Jn., 1 ; Jn., the sonne of a stranger, 3 ; the childe
of a !poore vagrant woman, 23 ; Marie the Daughtr of . . ., baseborne, 30 ; Robt., son of a stranger, 37 : Marie, the daughter of a
poore travayling Irishman, 40 ; Stephan, a strangr, 66 ; Richard a
stranger, 66, 75 ; a strang boy, 68, 73 ; a strang child, 86 ; Philip,
a strang., 69 ; Richard, a stra'gr, 69 ; Buried from the white a
maid, being a stranger, 70 ; a man, a stranger, 73, 74. 79*, 85, 100 ;
Urselley, the child of a stranger, 70 ; Luce, a strangr, 70 ; A stranger, 71,
77, 93, 102* ; a woman, a stranger, 72, 73, 81, 88, 90 : a gerle of Cornishs,
77 ; Thomas, a stranger, 92 ; the wyfe of Laurence, 78 ; Georg, a poore
vagrant boye, 95 ; a poore Boy, a stranger, 84 ; a poore man, 86 ; a poore
soldier, 87* ; Jean, a stranger, 88 ; a poore wandering boy called Griffyn,
90 ; a poore Irishma., 90 ; a poore Irish child, 91.

Aberrye, Ann, 56 ; Jul., 52.
Abraham (Abram), Ami, 65 ; Amos,
　10 ; Bennet, 65 ; Christoph., 20 ;
　Edm., 30, 65. 73 ; Edw., 23, 65 ;
　Ell., 13, 74 ; Grace, 27 ; Joan, 72 ;
　Jn., 14, 65, 74, 75 ; Margt., 45,
　62 ; Matth., 18, 45, 62 ; Phil:s,
　65 ; Rayn., 13, 14, 18, 20, 22, 23,
　25, 27, 30, 45, 77, 91 ; Sim., 22,
　77 ; Wm., 25.
Adams (Adames), Alice, 62 ; Jn., 47,
　98 ; My., 88 ; Robt., 98 ; Sus., 47.
Adie (Adye), —, 38 ; Ann, 69 ; Cath.,
　54 ; Eliz., 60 ; Joan. 33, 87 ; Jn.,
　37 ; Margt., 38 ; My., 36, 87 ;
　Margy, 91 ; Matth., 2, 32*, 33, 36,
　37, 85*, 87*, 88 ; Rich., 5, 69*,
　71 ; Rose, 81.
Adimer (Adymer, Adamer), Ann, 20 ;
　Joan, 56 ; Jan., 20, 22, 56 ; My.,
　22.
Allen (Allyn, Alyn), —, 23 ; Alice,
　53, 55 ; Avis, 11, 71 ; Christo., 11,
　84 ; Edw., 23, 52, 91 ; Isab., 52,
　68 ; Jn., 78 ; Margy., 58 ; My.,
　21 ; Matth., 9 ; Nich., 10, 72, 73 ;

Robt., 84 ; Rog., 7, 53 ; Rose, 7,
　69 ; Steph., 10, 72 ; Wm., 19*,
　21, 55.
Alrund. Rayn, 55 ; Thomasin, 55.
Amys, Parnell, 54.
Amytt, Gabr., 79 ; Robt., 79.
Anderson, Eliz., 64 ; Rich., 64.
Andrewes (Andrewe), Eliz., 62 ; Jn.,
　62 ; Sus., 98 ; Wm., 23*.
Anker, Jas., 2 ; Jn., 66.
Anncell, Alice, 58 ; My., 58.
Ansted, Jn., 82*.
A Powell, Hugh, 76.
Arctarie (Aritare), Eliz., 43, 94 ;
　Hen., 43, 94.
Ashton, Phebe, 60, 99 ; Wm., 60,
　99.
Athorn (Athourne, Atherne), Ann,
　63, 100 ; Dennis, 62 ; Dor., 60 ;
　Hen., 60, 62, 63.
Atkins, Bennet, 60.
Attur, Alice, 56.
Auinge, Joan, 99.
Austen, Jn., 73 ; Rog., 85.
Avice, Martha, 63.
Ayres, Robt., 1.

Bredge, Sar., 61.
Brenchlie, Jn., 51; Rich., 51.
Brenn, Thos., 24*, 78.
Brett (Breet), Joan, 13; Jn., 11; Mathie, 17, 75; Nich., 11, 17; Sus., 17.
Brewer, Ann, 11; Joan, 53; Thos., 11, 53.
Brice (Brise, Bryce), Mild., 55; Thos., 2, 74.
Brigen, Jn., 75.
Bridgman, My., 102.
Briston, Blance, 66.
Brockwell (Brockwoll, Breckwell), Dor., 49, 100; Grace, 36, 88*; Jas., 49; Joan, 60; Rich., 36, 37, 60, 88; Thomasin, 37; Wm., 70.
Broadstreet (Brodstreet, Brodstrete, Brodstreete, Bradstreet, Bradestreet), Alice, 41; Ann, 40; Christoph., 41, 42, 44*, 45; Dennice, 42; Edw., 7*, 12, 35, 44, 45, 53, 87, 91; Eliz., 7, 37, 53, 61, 64, 69, 70; Joan, 12, 41, 102; Jn., 7, 35, 37, 38*, 40, 41, 42, 44, 47, 87, 99*, 100; Sar., 47, 100; Son of, 99; Sus., 10, 42, 60.
Brome, My., 62.
Brooke (Broke),—,76; Agn.,68; Alice, 56, 58; Ann, 55, 76; Eliz., 13, 101; Joan, 51, 58, 61, 101; Jn., 50, 51, 65, 101; Lawr., 22, 25, 28, 55, 56, 58, 81*, 83, 85; Margt., 67, 69, 83; Margy., 3*; Marion, 11; Nath., 28, 81; Rich., 69; Robt., 76; Sus., 50; Thos., 25; Thomasin, 22, 61, 65; Wm., 11, 13, 28, 81*.
Brown (Browne), Alice, 54, 56; Christn., 53; Christop., 22; Eliz., 73; Hammon, 19; Joan, 26, 56; Jn., 17*, 75, 76; Mother, 78; Sus., 24, 62; Thos., 19, 22, 24, 26, 56, 84; Wid., 90; Wm., 56, 76.
Browninge, Christn., 62.
Bruke, Ann, 8; Edw., 2, 67.
Bryer, Jn., 70.
Bucke, Ann, 14, 15, 23, 78; Christn., 55, 80; Christop., 15; Hen., 12, 14, 16, 74; Jas., 14, 15, 18*, 20, 23, 55, 80; Joan, 14, 75; Jn., 13; Lawr., 11; Paul, 11, 13, 15, 17, 76; Pet., 16, 20, 23; Rich., 12; Sar., 23, 80; Thos., 17.
Buckmer, Reb., 59.
Buddle, Joan, 56.
Bulleye, Thos., 69.
Bunker, Rich., 83.
Burd (Byrd), Ann, 54; Dennis, 40, 90; Eliz., 40, 90; Jn., 40*, 90.

Burden, —, 39; Jn., 39.
Burdenson, Alice, 62.
Burge, Eliz., 53.
Burnell, Eliz., 71; Joan, 67; My., 71; Philip, 66; Seth., 52; Thos., 52, 67, 68.
Burton, Agn., 68; Joan, 55; Jn., 55.
Bush (Bushe), Ann, 19; Cath., 16, 79; Eliz., 27, 65; Jn., 65; Margt., 59; Wm., 14*, 16; 19, 27, 79, 85.
Butler, Matth., 36*.
Byx, Ann, 58.

Cacherell, Ann, 53.
Caco, Cornel, 79.
Cadman, Jn., 79.
Call, Eliz., 65; Jn., 65.
Carpenter, Dor., 98; Thos., 96.
Carr (Car, Carre), —, 23; Augusten, 42, 45, 47, 48, 98; Austin, 21, 42, 62, 65, 102; Jas., 5, 18, 21, 23, 25, 54, 55, 78*, 79; Jn., 8, 74, 78, 102; Margt., 54, 74; My., 25, 45, 55, 62, 65, 79, 102; Sar., 48; Sus., 5; Wm., 18, 47, 78, 98, 102.
Carter, Alice, 88; Ambr., 21; Cath., 25; Cirriack, 22; Eliz., 73, 85; Isaac, 19; Jn., 2, 15, 17, 19, 22, 24*, 25, 66, 78*, 88*; Margt., 6, 17, 56; Mathie, 15, 88; Rich. 4, 6, 73, 86; Thomasin, 89; Wm., 21.
Catell, Ann, 53.
Causey, Barnaby, 63; Eliz., 63.
Ceton, Adam, 66; Rabith, 66.
Chamberlen (Chamerlane), My., 64; Thos., 53; Wm., 64.
Channell, Hen., 70.
Chaplyne, Christn., 3.
Chapman, —, 90; Alle, 55; Christop., 52; Olive, 52.
Chappell, Alice, 92; Eliz., 28; Jas., 27, 80; Jn., 25, 27, 28, 35, 80*; My., 35; Prisc., 25, 80.
Charlton, Phebe, 62.
Chawker, Jn., 62; Lettice, 62.
Chillenden, —, 76; Alice, 12, 27, 73, 82; Ann, 19, 77; Edm., 29, 83; Edw., 25, 97; Eliz., 16, 22, 47; Isaac, 13, 75; Joan, 61; Jn., 11, 12, 14, 16, 18, 19, 20, 22*, 25, 27, 41, 42, 46*, 47, 61, 75, 81, 82, 94; Margt., 16, 59; Ralph, 14, 90; Sus., 18; Thos., 12, 42, 94*; Wm., 11, 12, 13, 16, 20, 22*, 29, 41, 54, 83, 85, 94; Zach., 54, 59.
Chorteose, Hen., 66.

Longley, Edw., 29, 83; Jean, 92; Joan, 58; Rich., 29.
Loue, Alex., 35; Alice, 40; Ann, 37; Arth., 88; Edw., 36, 37, 38, 39, 40, 42; Elean., 35; Eliz., 62; Geo., 32, 37, 42, 88; Grace, 38; Joan, 39; Thos., 32, 36; Walt., 42; Wm., 37.
Louker, Joan, 54.
Lowe, Eliz., 34, 58; Geo., 34; Jean, 81; Tim., 81.
Ludsom, Margy., 65; Randall, 65.
Luke, Joan, 53.
Lull, Avis, 2; Barb., 3; Joan, 52; Jn., 4, 68; Nich., 52.
Lyat, Margt., 53; Matth., 53.
Lye, Alice, 85; Ann, 81; Jn., 9, 71.
Lyffet, Mild., 57.

Mann (Man), Alice, 6; Ann, 53; Laur., 6, 53.
Mannering (Man'ering, Maneringe), —, 38, 39; Ann, 38; Isaac, 39; Wid., 97.
March (Marche, Marsh), —, 91; Eliz., 49; Jn., 49, 102.
Marshall (Mshall), Avis, 31, 47, 64; Dan., 23, 45, 46, 49, 51, 63, 96; Eliz., 46, 87; Esth., 63; Jas., 51; Jn., 67; Margt., 47; My., 49; Matth., 20, 23, 25*, 31, 45, 56, 81, 87, 89, 93*, 95, 96; Rich. 20, 89; Sus., 56, 81; Thos., 74.
Marth, Philis, 65.
Marten (Martyn), Jn., 84; Laur., 74; Thomasin, 60; Tim., 72.
Mashe, Avice, 64; Jn., 64.
Masters, Eliz., 15.
Matryce, Ann, 56.
Maxsted (Maxted), Alice, 58; Ann, 32, 59; Avis, 49; Cath., 47; child of, 95; Christop., 22; Dennis, 13, 15, 54, 62, 73; Edw., 7, 33, 36, 45, 47, 99; Eliz., 12, 15, 34, 52*, 58, 60, 74, 81, 87; Ell., 55, 95; Ezec., 25, 47, 49, 51, 63, 99; Jean, 29; Joan, 53, 71, 98; Jn., 9, 13, 25, 29, 30*, 32, 34*, 36, 38*, 46, 52, 58*, 81, 87, 89*; Margt., 10, 73; Martha, 63; Mild., 64*; Rayn., 13, 15, 17, 19, 22, 25, 34, 51; Renight, 51; Rich., 12, 15, 18, 20, 25, 47, 55*, 63, 95*, 99; Robt., 10, 18, 28, 31, 33, 44, 45, 46, 57, 59, 64, 73, 76, 81, 84, 97, 98*; Rose, 57; Sam., 17, 51; Sar., 44; Sus., 13, 28, 55, 61, 63, 73;

Thos., 20, 31, 38, 54, 81, 84, 89, 97; Thomasyn, 19; Wm., 7, 38, 53, 89.
May, Alice, 52; Joan, 4; Jn., 4, 52, 69.
Mayba'cke, Ann, 63, Thos., 63.
Meare (Meere, Meares, Mears, Mare, Mearse, Meerr, Meer), —, 27; Ann, 43, 47, 53, 93, 102; Cath., 63, 97; Eliz., 93; Joan, 44, 47, 62; Jn., 49; Leon, 43, 44, 47, 51*, 62, 93*, 94, 101; My., 27; Rebca, 62, 101; Son of, 94; Thomasin, 65; Wm., 47, 49, 63, 65, 97, 102.
Medowe, Eliz., 25; Jn., 25.
Mempas, Amy, 96; Thos., 96.
Mercer, —, 37; Thos., 37.
Merch (M'ch), Jn., 50; Pris., 50.
Metcaufe, Dav., 8.
Middleton, —, 21; Marian, 21.
Millen, Wm., 92.
Miller, Eliz., 93; Lawr., 93; Thomasin, 59.
Mills (Mylles), Alice, 11; Edw., 46 Geo., 86; Jn., 11, 46.
Mockett, Ann, 63; Jn., 63.
Mollenger, Jane, 48; Jeff., 44, 46, 48, 93; Nich., 46; Son of, 93*; Sus., 44.
Momforthe, Ann, 53.
Moon (Moone, Moune), Cath., 102; Christop., 45; Mich., 45, 102.
Moore (More), Andr., 54; Ann, 54, 74.
Moorcroft (Morecroste), —, 31; Ann, 63; Robt., 31.
Morton (Morto.), Augustie, 93; Lawr., 1.
Mosse, Jn., 69.
Mount (Mountt, Moont), Ann, 50; Dor., 60; Eliz., 38, 46, 65, 71, 97; Joan, 50, 61; Jn., 46, 50, 97; Margt., 51; Marian, 48; My., 39; Rich., 38*, 39, 40, 48, 50, 51, 99, 100, 101; Sar., 99; Son of, 100; Thos., 92; Walt., 38; Wm., 40, 101.
Murton, My., 55.

Napleton, Barb., 14; Jacob, 14, 15, 18, 21, 24, 26; Joan, 24; Jn., 26; Moses 15; Thos., 21; Wm., 18.
Nash, Mich., 92.
Natson, Hamon, 101.
Needes, Ann, 59.
Nester, Bennet, 62; Jn., 62.
Netter, Jn., 44; My., 44.

Phesant, Eliz., 60.
Phillipp, Eliz., 53.
Pickeforke (Pickeforks), —, 45; Jn.,
45, 97; Wm., 45, 97.
Pim (Pime, Pimb), Joan, 63, 103;
Steph., 45*, 63, 96*, 103; Wm.,
45.
Ping (Pynge), Ann, 40; Eliz., 99;
Geo., 93; Margt., 93; Wm., 40.
Pittell, Jn., 63; My., 63.
Place, Abrah., 36; Adam, 95; Alice,
6, 39, 65, 78*; Ann, 5, 35, 87;
Arth., 34, 86; Edw., 2, 37;
Elean., 7, 69; Eliz., 36, 38, 50,
64, 65; Ellise, 57; Hen., 24, 48,
50; Jas., 31, 48, 64, 101; Joan,
40, 54; Jn., 3, 8, 24, 27, 31, 33,
34, 35*, 36, 38, 39*, 40, 57, 86,
87, 95*, 98, 100; Joyce, 40, 43,
92; Mabel, 70; Margt., 54; My.,
33, 64, 95, 98, 100; Pet., 45, 65;
Phil., 2; Pris., 58; Ralph, 8, 69;
Son of, 99; Thos., 41; Thomasin,
33; Wm., 2, 4, 5*, 6*, 7, 9, 10,
11, 12, 14, 15, 16, 17, 19, 20, 21,
22, 23, 24, 25, 27*, 28, 29, 30*,
31, 32, 33*. 34, 35*, 36, 37*, 40,
41, 43, 45, 52, 54, 55, 56*, 57,
58*, 59, 67*. 68, 69, 71, 72, 73,
74, 76, 77, 78*, 79, 80, 81, 83, 84,
85, 99, 100, 103.
Plott, Jn., 55; Jul., 55.
Plummer, Isab., 66.
Pollard, Edw., 11, 12, 15, 19*, 72,
78; Joan, 12, 92; Jn., 11, 72;
My., 59; Mother, 95; Parn., 15,
76.
Pope (Poope), Ann, 22, 35, 41;
Cath., 84; Christop., 17; Cirriack,
40; Edw., 12, 60; Eliz., 8, 39,
44, 53, 90, 91; Geo., 42; Isab.,
59, 93; Jane, 15; Joan, 37, 88;
Jn., 7, 45, 70, 83; Margt., 90;
Matth., 11, 34, 35, 38, 43, 59, 62,
86, 93, 94, 95; Nich., 39, 91;
Rich., 48; Sar., 43, 62, 94;
Son of, 95; Steph., 12; Thos., 7, 11,
12, 15, 17, 22, 37, 38, 40, 41, 42,
44, 45, 48, 53, 83, 84, 88, 90*, 100;
Thomasin, 60; Wm., 34, 86.
Pordage, Alice, 99: Ann, 43, 102;
Daugh. of, 97; Eliz., 51; Joan,
48, 99; My., 64; Rich., 99;
Robt., 98; Thos., 43, 48, 51, 97,
99*, 102.
Porredge (Poredge, Porredg), Alice,
38, 69; Arth., 7, 70; Dor., 59;
Eliz., 2, 8, 52, 67; Grace, 39;
Hen., 3; Jos., 4; Marg., 8; My.,
36, 52, 57; Rich., 34, 72; Robt.,

5; Steph., 4, 5, 7, 52, 72; Thos.,
10, 34, 36, 38, 39, 40*, 42, 59, 67,
68; Thomsyn, 4; Wm., 42, 67.
Porter, Edw., 103; Eliz., 49; Jn.,
46; My., 44, 95; Mich., 44, 46,
49, 95, 100, 103; Son of, 100.
Potter, Sar., 59, 87; Thos., 59, 87.
Powell, Elean., 53, 81; Hen., 53;
Joan, 68.
Powne, Jn., 101; Marian, 101.
Preble (Preeble, Prebble, Prebell),
—, 30, 32; Ann, 32, 85; Edw.,
34, 37*; Ell., 59; Joan, 51; Jn.,
48, 85; Margt., 30; Thos., 48, 51,
59; Wm., 39*; Zach., 34.
Presson, Cath., 57; Isab., 12, 59;
Joan, 7; Jn., 72; Rich., 5;
Thos., 5; Wm., 12, 78.
Preston, Cath., 54; Joan, 53, 71;
Jn., 53, 66; Jul., 68; Wm., 54.
Price (Prise, Pryse, Pris), Dor., 43,
97; Greg., 41; Hen., 36; Jn., 37,
101; Math., 34*, 36, 37, 39. 41,
43, 45, 48, 97*; Mother, 101;
Pris., 48; Sar., 45, 97; Thos., 39.
Prior, Avis, 3.
Pryne, Alice, 56.
Purvior (Purvyor, Purviour), Margt.,
26; Sus., 57; Thos., 24*, 26, 57.
Pye, Ann, 58; Jn., 58.
Pysing, —, 86; Thos., 86.

Quilter, Eliz., 59.
Quoyfe, Mild., 64; Wm., 64.

Ragnold, Ann, 52.
Ran . . ., Eliz., 65.
Rand, Greg., 25; Rand., 25.
Rankorne, Namie, 64.
Rase, My., 59.
Rayner, Alice, 2, 67*; Ann, 21;
Avis, 14; Eliz., 32; Joan, 62;
Jn., 17, 61, 101; Margt., 77;
Sam., 14, 17, 21, 26, 30, 32, 83;
Sar., 26, 61, 83, 101: Wm., 30.
Raynerd (Raynard), Margt., 66;
Math., 68.
Reade, Jas., 99.
Raynolds (Raynold, Rainolds), Alice,
16, 76; Ann, 11; Avis, 13, 60;
Cath., 54; Christn., 54, 56;
Christop., 13, 15, 18, 31, 54;
Ciriack, 18; Edm., 12, 73; Edw.,
13; Geo., 28, 30, 32, 85; Hen.,
13, 26, 32, 54; Joan, 54, 61; Jn.,

Whitesyde, Elle., 57.
Wiget, My., 88.
Wiggall, Thos., 70.
Wihall, Christn., 55.
Wilcox (Wylcockes, Wilcocke), Joan, 52; Wm., 66.
Wild (Wilde), Bennet, 63; Eliz., 47, 98; Joan, 47, 98.
Wiles, Margt., 74.
Williams, Ann, 62, 63; Rich., 62, 94.
Willoway, My., 56; Rich., 56.
Wills (Wylls), —, 69; Elean., 58; Jn., 70; Margt., 8; Thomasin, 70.
Wilson, —, 33; Bethulia, 61; Sol., 61; Thos., 33.
Wingfield (Wingfeield, Wynckfild, Winckfeld), Ann, 22; Cath., 61; Geo., 20; Joan, 100; My., 56; Matth., 21; Thos., 97; Walt., 92; Wm., 18*, 20, 21, 22.
Wise (Wisse, Wyse), Clem., 39; Edw., 61; Joan, 63; Jn., 97;

Margy., 37; Sar., 61; Wm., 37, 39, 95, 97.
Wollet, Rich., 87.
Wood, —, 1, 90; Abrah., 96; Alice, 49, 90; Benj., 61; Edw., 48; Eliz., 28, 51, 64, 99; Grace, 98; Joan, 59, 61; Nich., 27, 30, 80, 84; Rich., 1, 32, 48, 49, 51, 64; Sus., 57, 96; Thos., 37; Walt., 40; Wm., 27, 28, 30, 32, 34*, 37, 40, 80, 84, 94.
Woodwall, Alice, 88; Amy, 90, 91; Ann. 40, 46, 53, 65, 98; Eliz., 17, 46, 88, 89; Francis, 42; Joan, 61; Jn., 9, 13, 17, 39, 53, 75, 91; Josias, 38; My., 41; Matthias, 8; Matth., 38, 39*, 41, 42, 89, 91*, 92; Nich., 46, 98; Sar., 13, 39, 61; Thomasin, 10, 90.
Woollan, Mild., 55; Thos., 55.
Wylmontnige, Margt., 54.
Wyman, Joan, 72; Steph., 72.

RECTORS AND VICARS.

Allen, Thomas, V., xi.
Andrewe, Rich., V., ix.
Audenard, Egidius de, R., vii.
Baker, John, V., x.
Barber, John, V., ix.
Barton, David, V., xi.
Bassett, Albert, V., x.
Bassett, George, V., x.
Baterman, Thos., V., ix.
Belle, John, V., ix.
Beklesfeld (Bekenesfeld), Laur. de, V., ix.
Benyngton, John, V., ix.
Boodle, John Adolphus, V., xii.
Bowyer, John, V., ix.
Brito, Ranulphus, R., vii.
Browne, Adam, V., ix.
Cassell, Giles, V., ix.
Caunvyll, Jordan de, R., viii.
Charleton, Joh. de, R., vii.
Conold, John, V., xi.
Dalton, John, V., x.
Derby, Henry de, R., viii.
Ellis, Peter, V., ix.
Ellison, Stanhope, V., xi.
Faversham, Thos. Edm. de, V., viii.
Gamlyn, John, V., xi.
Harding, Richard, V., x.
Heaton, Henry, V., xi.
Hill, Hercules, V., x.
Holland, Philip, V., x.
Houghton, Thos., V., ix.
Johnson, John, V., xi.

Knovyle, Mich. de, R., vii.
Langham, John, V., ix.
Langwath, John, V., ix.
Layton, Edw., V., ix.
Lee, Edw. Henry, V., xii.
Leycester, Thos. de, R., viii.
Lymsey, Roger, V., x.
Mackallar, John V., x.
Meopham, Rich., R., viii.
Monde, Thos., V., viii.
Moore, Charles, V., xi.
Newman, Robt., V., ix.
Place, William, V., x.
Plees, William, V., xi.
Radcliffe, Percival V., xi.
Sto. Leofardo, Gilb. de, R., vii.
Sardynia, Wm. de, R., vii.
Seyliard, Thos., V., x.
Shene, Rich., V., ix.
Skene, Robert, V., xi.
Smith, Samuel, V., x.
Sponar, Edw., V., ix.
Spooner, Henry Maxwell, V., xii.
Stony Stretford, John de, V., ix.
Strenge, Laurence, V., ix.
Taylor, Thomas, V., x.
Thompson, Robert, V., x.
Turvyll, Philip de, R., viii.
Wayte, William, V., ix.
White, Sam., Geo. Booth, V., xii.
Whitman, John, V., ix.
Weighte, Thos. Wm., V., xi.
Wuluinus, R., vii.

THE   REGISTERS

OF

BOUGHTON-UNDER-BLEAN,

CO. KENT.

Issued to Subscribers By
THE PARISH REGISTER SOCIETY.
1903.

REGISTERS PRINTED.

1896.
1. BANSTEAD, SURREY.
2. WORCESTER, ST. ALBANS, WORCESTERSHIRE.
3. BEER HACKETT, DORSET.
4. NORTH LUFFENHAM, RUTLAND.
5. MONK FRYSTON, YORKSHIRE.

1897.
*6. STRATFORD-ON-AVON (baptisms), WARWICKSHIRE.
7. IPSWICH, ST. NICHOLAS, SUFFOLK.
8. UPTON, BERKSHIRE.
9. HAYDOR, LINCOLN.
10. NEWENDEN, KENT.
11. KIRK ELLA, YORKSHIRE.

1898.
12. WALESBY, NOTTINGHAMSHIRE.
13. SARNESFIELD, HEREFORDSHIRE.
14. DODDINGTON-PIGOT, LINCOLNSHIRE.
15. BISHAM, BERKSHIRE.
*16. STRATFORD-ON-AVON (marriages), WARWICKSHIRE.

1899.
17. LYDLINCH, DORSET.
18. LEDBURY, HEREFORDSHIRE.
19. BATTLEFIELD, SHROPSHIRE.
20. SIBDON CARWOOD, SHROPSHIRE.
21. ROWINGTON, WARWICKSHIRE.
22. SHIPTON, SHROPSHIRE.
23. HARLEY, SHROPSHIRE.
24. MELVERLEY, SHROPSHIRE.
25. CLYST ST. GEORGE, DEVONSHIRE.
26. SMETHCOTE, SHROPSHIRE.

1900.
27. CRESSAGE, SHROPSHIRE.
28. SHEINTON, SHROPSHIRE.
29. FORD, SHROPSHIRE.
*30. A LIST OF PARISH REGISTERS.
31. PITCHFORD, SHROPSHIRE.
32. BITTON, GLOUCESTERSHIRE.
33. UPTON IN OVERCHURCH, CHESHIRE.
34. MORE, SHROPSHIRE.

1901.
35. STAPLETON, SHROPSHIRE.
36. HUGGATE, YORKSHIRE.
37. MORDEN, SURREY.
38. CLUNBURY, SHROPSHIRE.
39. MORETON CORBET, SHROPSHIRE.
40. HOPTON CASTLE, SHROPSHIRE.
41. HUGHLEY, SHROPSHIRE.

1902.
42. MERSTHAM, SURREY.
43. HEADON, NOTTINGHAMSHIRE.
44. TARRANT HINTON, DORSET.

1903.
45. CANON FROME, HEREFORDSHIRE.
46. MUNSLEY, HEREFORDSHIRE.
47. MOULTON, NORTHAMPTONSHIRE.
48. COLEBY, LINCOLNSHIRE.
49. BOUGHTON-UNDER-BLEAN, KENT.

PROSPECTIVE WORK.

1. TOTTERNHOE, BEDFORDSHIRE.
2. SWETTENHAM, CHESHIRE.
3. REPTON, DERBYSHIRE.
4. PLYMTREE, DEVONSHIRE.
5. WILLESDEN, MIDDLESEX.
6. LEIGH, STAFFORDSHIRE.
7. IPSWICH, ST. MATTHEW, SUFFOLK.
8. EAST GRINSTEAD, SUSSEX.
9. WESTBOURNE, SUSSEX.
10. MADDINGTON, WILTSHIRE.
11. STRATFORD-ON-AVON (burials) WARWICKSHIRE.
12. LEDBURY (continuation), HEREFORDSHIRE.

AND OTHERS.

* Additional copies of Volumes 6 and 16 at 10s. 6d. each, and of Volume 30 at 5s., can be obtained from the Hon. Secretary, Mr. E. A. Fry, 172, Edmund Street, Birmingham.

Miscellanea Genealogica
et Heraldica.

Illustrated with Facsimiles of Grants of Arms and Old Charters in Colours, Armorial Book Plates, Seals, Autographs, etc.

EDITED BY W. BRUCE BANNERMAN, F.S.A.

NEW SERIES, Vols. I., II., III. and IV., price £1 1s. each, in cloth, or £4 the set. Comprising Memoranda relating to more than 1,000 Families. Illustrated with upward of 500 Armorial Bookplates, Engravings of Arms, Autographs, Seals, etc. The back Numbers of this Series are on Sale, price 9d. each. Indexes, etc., 5s. each. Cases, 2s.

SECOND SERIES, Vols. I. II., III., IV. and V., price £1 5s. each, or £5 10s. the set; the Volume contains Numbers for Two Years. Indexes, etc., to each Volume separately, price 5s. Cases, 2s. Back Numbers of this Series, price 1s. each.

THIRD SERIES, Vols. I., II., III. and IV., price £1 5s. each. Now continuing in Quarterly Parts, price 2s. 6d. each.

Subscription, 10s. 6d. per Annum, post free.

INDEXES, ETC., 5s. EACH.   CASES, 2s.

London: MITCHELL & HUGHES, 140, Wardour Street, W.

***

A Digest of the Parish Registers
WITHIN THE DIOCESE OF WORCESTER,
Issued by the Committee of Parish Registers,
By Authority of the WORCESTER DIOCESAN CONFERENCE.

This Digest has been prepared under the direction of a Committee appointed at the Diocesan Conference, held at Birmingham, in 1896, and has been completed from the original Returns supplied by the Incumbents of the Parishes within the Diocese. The dates when each Volume of Registers commence and end, the number of leaves, material on which they are written, and the size and general condition, are all clearly stated under each parish.

Added to all this useful information, is a table showing for what years in every parish the Bishops Transcripts, previous to 1700, are now in existence in Edgar Tower, Worcester.

As only a limited number of copies has been printed, early application is necessary to secure a copy.

***

The Midland Educational Company, Ltd., Corporation St., Birmingham.
Price, 5s. Nett; Post Free.

THE BRITISH RECORD SOCIETY, LTD.,

Publishes, Quarterly, *The Index Library*,

Containing:—

CALENDARS OF WILLS IN THE PREROGATIVE COURT OF CANTERBURY, also of those in the Probate Registries of LICHFIELD, BLANDFORD, NORTHAMPTON, BERKSHIRE, GLOUCESTER, LEICESTER, BRISTOL, EDINBURGH, etc.

CALENDARS OF CHANCERY PROCEEDINGS.

ABSTRACTS OF INQUISITIONES POST-MORTEM FOR LONDON, GLOUCESTERSHIRE, WILTSHIRE, etc.

Annual Subscription, £1. 1s. Prospectus and full particulars from the Hon. Sec., E. A. FRY, 172, EDMUND STREET, BIRMINGHAM.

Notes and Queries for Somerset and Dorset,

Edited by FREDERIC WILLIAM WEAVER, M.A., Milton Clevedon, Evercreech, Somerset Editor of "Visitations of the Counties of Somerset and Hereford" and "Somerset Incumbents," and CHARLES HERBERT MAYO, M.A., R.D., Vicar of Long Burton, near Sherborne, Canon non-res. of Sarum, author of "Bibliotheca Dorsetiensis,"

Vol. VI. commenced March, 1898. Parts issued quarterly. Subscriptions 5s. per annum, payable in advance to either of the Editors, to whom all literary and business communications should be addressed.

NOW READY : upwards of 200 pages, cloth. Price 3s. 6d.

A Supplement to How to Write the History of a Family,

By W. P. W. PHILLIMORE, M.A., B.C.L.

The First and Second Editions have been long since quite exhausted. Much additional information of practical value has been gathered together since the handbook was issued, and this has been put together in the form of a separate supplement, so that it may be available for the possessors of each edition. The supplement matches the original work.

I contains amongst other matter a Chapter for Beginners, Chapters on Scotch and Irish Genealogy and Records, which have been revised by Lyon King of Arms, Ulster King of Arms, and the Deputy Keeper of the Public Records, Ireland, and revised Lists of Probate Registries (England, Scotland, and Ireland) and Marriage Licenses, etc.

PUBLISHED BY W. P. W. PHILLIMORE, 124, CHANCERY LANE, W.C.

Date Due

All library items are subject to recall at any time.

MAY 0 3 2010		

CPSIA information can be obtained
at www.ICGtesting.com
Printed in the USA
BVHW08s0847060818

523682BV00022B/1021/P